The Arizona Bar Exam

Pass It Now

SECOND EDITION

Chad Noreuil
CLINICAL PROFESSOR OF LAW
SANDRA DAY O'CONNOR COLLEGE OF LAW
ARIZONA STATE UNIVERSITY

CAROLINA ACADEMIC PRESS
Durham, North Carolina

Library of Congress Cataloging-in-Publication Data

Noreuil, Chad.
The Arizona bar exam : pass it now / Chad Noreuil. -- 2nd ed.
p. cm.
Includes index.
ISBN 978-1-61163-078-7 (alk. paper)
1. Bar examinations--Arizona. I. Title.

KFA2476.N67 2011
340.076--dc23

2011024509

Carolina Academic Press
700 Kent Street
Durham, North Carolina 27701
Telephone (919) 489-7486
Fax (919) 493-5668
www.cap-press.com

Printed in the United States of America

FOR ZEN

... the love of my life, my heart & soul,
my inspiration, my greatest teacher, my son.

Contents

Acknowledgments

Special thanks to Arizona Supreme Court Chief Justice Rebecca White Berch, Amy Levine, Jenny Bishop, Mike Jones, Marie Ann Lambert, Maddi Vera, Harmony Simmons, Ben Herbert, and Natalya Ter-Grigoryan for all of your efforts in helping make this book become a reality. Thank you all!

The Arizona Bar Exam

1

Taking the Arizona Bar Exam

Three years of hazing and the rat race known as law school, and now this—the bar exam. You've barely had time to celebrate graduating, and now you have to learn (or re-learn) a LOT of law in a relatively short amount of time. Worse still, if you don't pass, all of that debt you accumulated over the last three years is basically for nothing. Ugh. So the first thing I'll say is this: you've got to get over the "why in the heck do I have do this" mentality.

There actually is a valid reason for taking the exam. As the National Conference of Bar Examiners puts it, there is a bar exam requirement in order to protect the public. And it's true in this regard—there does need to be a minimum level of competency to represent clients, some of whom are literally entrusting their lives to a licensed attorney. A two-day exam may not be the best way to ensure this level of competency, but it's the process that everyone has to go through. So if you want your license to practice law, the bar exam just became one of the most important things in your life.

Of course, to actually be admitted to practice law in Arizona, you must also pass The Multistate Professional Responsibility Exam (MPRE), and a Character and Fitness evaluation. For more information on either of these requirements, you can visit http://www.supreme.state.az.us/admis/ or contact the committee at the number or address below.

Committee on Examinations
Supreme Court of Arizona
1501 West Washington St.
Phoenix, AZ 85007-3231
Telephone: (602) 364-0371

The Exam Itself

The Arizona bar exam is offered twice a year—once in February and once in July. The two-day exam is always administered on the last Tuesday and Wednesday of that particular month. Beginning with the July 2011 bar examination, the first day of the Arizona bar examination will consist of six essay questions (rather than the twelve that have traditionally been tested) and two Multistate Performance Test (MPT) questions. Essays will include up to six Multistate Essay Examination (MEE) questions but could include Arizona law questions. The MPT is a new addition to the exam and will consist of two 90-minute sessions, with one problem per session. For the MPT, you will be given a "library" of cases/statutes/facts and asked to write a legal document, such as an office memo or persuasive court brief.

The following subject matter areas may be tested on the essay portion of the exam: business associations; conflict of laws; contracts; torts; criminal law; constitutional aspects of criminal procedure; trusts; wills; professional responsibilities; civil procedure; constitutional law; evidence; real property; Uniform Commercial Code; family law; and community property. (Note: family law and conflicts of law are "new" subjects added to this list that have not been previously tested.) In addition to those subjects listed above, applicants may be tested on any subject matter listed by the National Conference of Bar Examiners as areas of law to be tested on the Multistate Essay Examination. Questions will be unlabeled and not necessarily limited to one subject matter.

The second day of the exam will remain the same and consist of 200 Multistate Bar Examination (MBE) multiple choice questions (100 questions during the three-hour morning session and 100 questions during the three-hour afternoon session). The grading breakdown will now be as follows: 50% for the MBE (multiple choice) portion of the exam, 30% for the essay portion of the exam, and 20% for the MPT portion of the exam. For grading purposes, Arizona combines and scales all sections for a total of 600 points. In order to be deemed successful on the Arizona Bar Exam (or in other words, in order to "pass"), an applicant must achieve a combined score of 410 or higher.

Handwriting the Essays vs. Typing the Essays

When I tutor, I am often asked: should I handwrite or type my essays? The answer: whichever you are most accustomed to using. If you wrote out your exams during law school, you should probably write out your bar exam essays. If you typed your law school exams, then you'll most likely want to type the bar exam. Whichever you choose, just make sure you practice the same way. You don't want to practice writing essays, and then type them the day of the exam (or vice-versa).

If you write your answers—write legibly! This should go without saying, but the bigger point here is to think about how you are going about practicing your essays. Anyone can write legibly during a single 30-minute essay, but the true test is how you write when your hand/arm/body/mind is fatigued. If the grader cannot read your answer, you cannot get credit for it. As such, it's key to practice writing out multiple essays in a row to see how your legibility holds up under stress.

If you use a computer, make sure it is functioning well. Take it into a computer shop and have it checked out. It will be worth the investment. I recently tutored someone whose computer failed during the second essay question. Needless to say, it wasn't a pleasant experience. If you choose to use a laptop, you should know that you will be required to load specific software onto your computer. Here is the information on computers provided by the Arizona Bar Examiners Committee (found at their official website, with the specific link below): http://www.supreme.state.az.us/admis/examinfo.htm#EXAMINATION%20INFORMATION

Applicants will be permitted to use their personal laptops for the essay portion if all requirements are met, and they have downloaded the required software. This option is available *only* at the main examination site, at the discretion of the Committee, and dependent upon site and software availability. The fee is $125. Use of typewriters, other laptops or electronic aid(s) is not permitted for standard testing.

SofTest may only be used on a personal laptop. It is compatible with Macintosh operating systems. Please review system requirements on the ExamSoft website: www.examsoft.com/barfaq.

If you have filed a laptop registration form you will be provided information, via email, on the required procedures to download and register the SofTest software onto your laptop. Even if you have previously registered SofTest on your laptop for the Arizona bar exam, other jurisdictions, or law school, you must complete these registration requirements. Do not attempt to pre-register on a previously used ExamSoft website.

No laptop positions will be held in advance, nor does previous use of a laptop automatically carry to a subsequent examination.

After the bar examination, you will upload your essay answers to the ExamSoft server. The Committee on Examinations will retrieve your morning and afternoon essay files for printing and distribution for grading. Your computer must be available for at least fourteen days after the exam in the event the Committee or ExamSoft require access to your hard drive.

2

Preparing for the Journey

Above All Else—Keep a Positive Mental Outlook

Granted, given the nature of the beast you are about to confront, keeping a positive mental outlook can be a difficult task. But I'd like to make this as clear as possible at the outset: in my humble opinion, having a positive mental outlook is the single most important thing you can do in order to pass the bar exam. Numerous studies have shown that optimists learn more efficiently.[1]

Whatever you have to do to remain positive, do it. Believe you will pass; start telling yourself every single day that you will pass; put notes up around your house reminding you to stay positive; visualize yourself opening the letter from the Bar Examiners telling you that you passed. I cannot guarantee that you will pass if you do this. But I can guarantee that your likelihood of success is much higher by being positive and believing you will pass than by being

---

1. *See* Sarath A. Nonis, Gail I. Hudson, Melodie J. Philhours, & Joe K. Teng, *Changes in College Student Composition and Implications for Marketing Education: Revisiting Predictors of Academic Success*, 58 J. of Bus. Res. 321, 327 (2005) (results show successful students exhibit high level of drive and optimism); Rachel Seginer, *Defensive Pessimism and Optimism Correlates of Adolescent Future Orientation*, 15 J. of Adolescent Res. 307, 317 (2000) (optimism had positive links with the motivational component of prospective education); *see generally* Peter Schulman, *Applying Learned Optimism to Increase Sale Productivity*, 19 J. of Pers. Selling & Sales Mgmt. 31 (1999) (expectation that one will succeed affects performance).

negative and having doubts. You WILL pass—believe it, achieve it.

How do you stay positive, stay motivated during the process? Why are you taking the exam in the first place? A better life for you? A better life for your kids? To help people? To make a lot of money? Remind yourself of why you went to law school—that may help. If not, find other motivations. At the very least, you've likely forgotten most everything you learned in law school, so take this opportunity to actually learn the law—because you can bet the house that family and friends will be calling for legal advice down the road. ☺

Your Personal Relationships during the Bar Exam

Approach the bar exam as if it's your full-time job. It's absolutely critical to communicate with friends and family that you may not have time to hang out with them or return calls during the lead-up to the bar exam. The bar exam is tough enough without having drama with family and friends, so explain to them the rigorous study demands that you'll be forced to endure and ask for support (and sympathy!).

Moreover, explain the importance of the exam, as some non-lawyers may not even realize that you cannot practice law until you pass the bar exam. Finally, it may be a good idea to apologize in advance if you appear stressed out when you do interact with family and friends. This is not to say that you shouldn't take a break once in a while, but your "breaks" will likely be less frequent than the "breaks" you took during your last year of law school (the so-called "bored to death" year of law school).

If friends and family miss you too much, get them involved: ask them to help you. This may be in the form of cooking a few meals, doing your laundry, or even helping you study. Some of you learn best by talking through things, so consider having your significant other act as a sounding board for your recitation of rules, or perhaps have him/her go through flashcards with you.

Lifestyle during the Bar Exam

In addition to your personal relationships, your lifestyle will be a significant factor in whether you pass the bar exam. Diet, exercise, and adequate sleep are key factors to having your brain function at its optimal level. First—diet. You are what you eat, or so the saying goes. Translation: if you eat Ding Dongs, then you are going to be a ding-dong.

To maximize your ability to learn (e.g., to process and retain information) it's critical to eat healthy, well-balanced meals. Eat all natural foods (fruits, vegetables, whole grains, lean proteins, etc.) and cut out processed foods and sugar as much as possible. Sugar in particular can have a deleterious effect on brain function,[2] as can too much caffeine.[3]

Conversely, incorporate some Omega 3 and/or Omega 6 fatty acids into your diet, most commonly found in fish. If you don't like fish, there are a variety of supplements that you can take. Recent studies have shown that Omega 3 fatty acids improve brain function—especially memory.[4] Salmon, mackerel, herring, trout, tuna, and halibut are foods rich in Omega 3 fatty acids.

---

2. Jane A. Goldman et al., *Behavioral Effects of Sucrose on Preschool Children*, 14 J. of Abnormal Child Psychol. 565 (1986) (study found objective evidence in young children of a significant time-dependent behavior effect of sucrose ingestion).

3. BBC.news.com, Caffeine 'Reduces Productivity', http://news.bbc.co/uk/1/hi/health/1142492.stm (last visited Nov. 17, 2009) (study found high caffeine intake leads to dehydration that, coupled with stimulating effects of caffeine, causes detrimental effect on concentration).

4. *See* S. Yehuda, S. Rabinovitz, & D.I. Mostofsky, *Essential Fatty Acids and the Brain: From Infancy to Aging*, 26 Neurobiology of Aging S98, S100 (2005) ("In general, EFA [essential fatty acids] improves learning and memory." (citing S. Yehuda, S. Rabinovitz, R.L. Carasso, & D.I. Mostof-

Bar Review Courses

If you are preparing to take the bar exam, you have no doubt heard of the many bar review courses during your time in law school. Generally speaking, bar review courses are a good idea, if for no other reason than they force you to attend classes. Moreover, many of them give you outlines and/or practice questions (for both the essay portion and the MBE). It could also afford you an opportunity to meet a lot of potential study partners (particularly if you are taking the bar in a state different from the one where you went to school).

Of course, there are many people who do not take bar review courses and still pass the bar exam. Money is always a consideration, but passing is always more important than more debt, right? Bar review courses are good at doing one thing in particular—getting you on a schedule to attend classes. Research what is available in the area of bar review courses and see which one is best for you as far as money, location, materials, and your learning style.

Staying Focused and Staying Motivated

Staying focused and motivated is absolutely critical to success on the bar exam (which is why I'm discussing it again in more depth). It's also one of the toughest things to do for the laborious

---

sky, *Mixture of Essential Fatty Acids Rehabilitates Stress Effects on Learning, and Cortisol and Cholesterol Level*, 101 INT'L J. NEUROSCIENCE 73–87 (2000))); John Hopkins Health Alerts, Eating Fish May Help Preserve Your Memory (Along with Your Heart) and Protect Against Alzheimer's Disease (June 13, 2006), http://www.johnshopkinshealthalerts.com/alerts/nutrition_weight_control/JohnsHopkinsNutritionWeightControlHealthAlert_208-1.html (recent study found eating fish with Omega-3 fatty acids twice a week reduces the risk of developing Alzheimer's disease by seventy percent).

two-month study process. The key is to be aware when you are getting in a funk. When your "down" energy times hit (and they will for virtually everyone), be aware that it's happening, accept it, and step back for a second. Remind yourself of how important this exam is to your life.

First, you didn't go through three years of law school for the heck of it. Remind yourself why you went to law school every chance you get. Whatever the reason(s)—more money, better quality of life, helping people—remind yourself of these reasons during the unmotivated times. Your law degree won't be worth much unless you pass the exam. The more you remind yourself of this, the more likely you will be able to stay motivated.

The Zen of Passing the Bar Exam

There is an old Zen saying: the root of all suffering is resisting what is. Nothing is right or wrong, good or bad—it just is. Here is something I tell my students before final exams: life always boils down to two things—"Get To" or "Have To." Everything you do can be compartmentalized into these two categories. The more you choose to place your perspective in the "get to" column, the better your attitude will be (and, as we have already seen, a positive attitude is a definite factor in maximizing your study time's effectiveness).

At some point, you may find yourself saying that you "have to" take the bar exam. Those who have been denied admittance to law school (or those who have flunked out or withdrawn) likely would say you "get to" take the exam (while they do not). Taking the exam is a privilege—one which you had to trudge through three years of law school to earn. Remind yourself that you don't "have to" study—you "get to" study, because you are afforded the opportunity to see, to read, to understand.

If you are reading this at the beginning stages of your bar exam experience, it may not have much of an impact. But when you find yourself unmotivated, go back and read the last two sections—see if it helps. You don't "have to" take the bar exam, you "get to" take it. The more you appreciate this fact (and everything else in your life), the more likely it is that you will pass the exam. And the happier you will be throughout the journey. [For a more comprehensive discussion on this topic, feel free to check out one of my other books, *The Zen of Passing the Bar Exam* (Carolina Academic Press, 2010).]

It's a Marathon, Not a Sprint

Yes, you have a lot of information to absorb, and a lot of "practicing" to do. But part of the process is making sure you take a break every now and then. A run-down body and mind is not optimal for learning. Accordingly, be sure to take a break at regular intervals—both throughout the day, and by taking entire days off. Do something to give your mind and body a rest. Hopefully, you will come back to your study schedule refreshed.

Fight the temptation to feel guilty about taking a break (so long, of course, as your breaks aren't taking up more time than studying). Breaks are vital to the process—so when you take one, resist the temptation to start going over "rules" in your head. The best way to combat this is to do something that truly takes your mind away from studying. A word to the wise—if you rent a movie on your night off, just make sure it's not a legal thriller.

3

Learning the Law

Know Yourself

What kind of learner are you? How do you learn best? If you don't know, try to figure it out in order to be most efficient when studying. Of course, we are all a combination of learners, but some are more visual, others more auditory, etc. After your 20 years (or more) of school, hopefully you have some idea of what type of learner you are. If not, experiment. See what works best for you. Try flashcards, audiotapes, explaining rules of law to your significant other, memorizing your outline while walking, etc. Oftentimes, a combination of the above may work best—especially when you want to alleviate the potential boredom of the same exact routine.

If you are really at a loss as to what type of learner you are, there are various websites you can go to in order to figure it out.[5] Regardless of how you study, the most important thing is to be focused, be present. The more you are able to concentrate on the task at hand, the more information you will retain.

When I tutor for the bar exam, I am often asked, "How do I learn all of this law? What's the best way to learn the actual rules?" Aside from knowing what type of learner you are and experimenting with different study techniques, you will learn most of the law by

---

5. Grace Fleming, About.com, Learning Style Quiz: Visual, Kinesthetic, and Auditory Styles, http://homeworktips.about.com/od/homeworkhelp/a/lstyleqz.htm (last visited Nov. 17, 2009).

creating your own outlines. If you utilize a bar review course, you may have outlines provided to you, but you should still create your own for each subject.

One reason to create your own outlines: the bar review course outlines may not be organized in a way that is most conducive to how you learn best. The manner in which you process a subject's interrelation may be different from the bar review outlines (and/or a peer's outlines that may have been given to you). Moreover, creating your own outlines will engage you in active learning, which will reinforce the learning process. (More on this in the next section.)

Ultimately, your goal is to be able to literally re-create your outlines from memory. In an ideal world, when you are actually taking the exam, you would want to go through a "mental checklist" of each topic to "cross reference" against the fact pattern. This will greatly aid you in issue spotting during the exam. Think about it—if you can mentally picture your outline (and the rules that go with it), taking the exam will be like taking an open book exam!

Granted, being able to mentally recall most or all of each outline is a difficult task. But it is not an impossible task. The more you are able to focus/visualize/be present when creating your outlines (and later going through them), the better off you will be.

Mnemonics

Of course, you can always use mnemonics to help you remember certain things. Here is one of my favorites that a former student I tutored came up with regarding the possible defenses to contract enforcement: **DUI IS DUM**

Duress
Undue Influence
Incapacity

Illegality
Statute of Frauds

Deception (misrepresentation)
Unconscionability
Mistake

Here is another of my favorite mnemonics. This one comes from Criminal Procedure and notes the eight exceptions to the warrant requirement. And you should be able to remember it—because only an "ESCAPIST" can beat a valid search and seizure.

Exigent Circumstances
Search Incident to Arrest
Consent
Automobile
Plain View
Inventory
Special Needs (school searches, border searches, etc.)
Terry "Stop and Frisk"

The Energy Notebook

Aside from the techniques I have already referred to, I often recommend an "energy notebook" for learning all of the rules of law. Get a notebook—make it a special notebook. Put pictures of your family, pets, favorite people or things on the front, and give the notebook positive energy. (If you have kids or a significant other, a great thing to do is have them write in the notebook on the inside cover.) Yes—I'm serious about this. The notebook has to be one of reverence and positive energy (or you will more easily grow to resent it, which will only undermine your learning).

Most people review their outlines when they try to learn the law. They will go through a particular subject and try to repeat the rule of law for the particular sub-topics. Often, especially early on, you won't get all of the rules correct. That's when the energy notebook comes into play. Every time you "miss" a rule of law, write it down verbatim in your notebook.

This process forces your mind to work on different levels, thereby increasing your likelihood of remembering the full rule next time around. Specifically, it forces you into active learning—recalling the rule and physically writing it down. The physical act of writing out the rule calls upon the brain to engage on a second level (rather than just reading the rule you missed), which adds strength to your brain's neurotransmitters (and thus makes it more likely that you will remember the rule in the future).

Always write down the date and subject in your notebook when you start your "rule learning" session. This will give you a good idea of where you stand as you get closer to exam day because you can immediately tell how much of the law you still don't know (and how much you do know) at various intervals of studying. In an ideal world, the number of rules you write in your notebook will be far fewer than what you wrote down early in the process.

Moreover, the energy notebook will be a good study aid in the final week of the exam. Rather than trying to review your (potentially) lengthy outlines a day or days before the exam, you can just review the rules in the recent entries of your notebook. Do note that, at first, it may be a daunting task to memorialize the rules you "miss" by writing them all down, but if you stick with it, you should find that you are learning all the rules faster than when you were just reading over your outlines. Also, I wouldn't suggest starting to write entries into your notebook until you are at least relatively familiar with the particular subject you are studying.

Get on a study schedule and stick to it. The brain learns best when you study at the same time every day. The best time to study is at the same times as the bar exam (from 9–12 and 2–5), to prepare your brain to function at the time it's most important. Of course, you will likely want to study at night as well, but be sure you are engaging your brain during the actual bar exam hours. (Some of these hours will likely be during a bar review course, so make sure you are not "zoning out" during these lectures.)

Find a comfortable place to study—a sanctuary where distractions are minimal. It may help to try different places (library, coffee shop, your bedroom), but the key is having a set-up that allows you to focus on the task at hand.

4

The Arizona Essay Exam

As I noted in Chapter 1, there are six (6) essays in Arizona. The first day of the exam will be the essay day. You will be given thirty (30) minutes to complete each essay. Although there are only six essays given, the following subjects are all subjects that could potentially be tested: business associations; conflict of laws; contracts; torts; criminal law; constitutional aspects of criminal procedure; trusts; wills; professional responsibilities; civil procedure; constitutional law; evidence; real property; Uniform Commercial Code; family law; and community property. (Note: family law and conflicts of law are "new" subjects added to this list.) In addition to those subjects listed above, applicants may be tested on any subject matter listed by the National Conference of Bar Examiners as areas of law to be tested on the Multistate Essay Examination ("MEE"). Questions will be unlabeled and not necessarily limited to one subject matter.

Although most (if not all) of the six essay questions will be MEE questions (drafted by the NCBE), applicants should still note relevant Arizona law distinctions for each essay. MEE questions tend to be more specific, whereas previous Arizona essay questions tended to be more "open-ended" issue spotting type of questions. Accordingly, it's important to be familiar with both types of questions.

Scoring

The essay portion of the exam counts for 30% of your overall score. Each essay is graded on a scale of zero (0) to six (6), with six (6) being the highest possible score on any one essay. Here is a breakdown of the scoring, as given by the Arizona Committee on Examinations.

NUMERICAL SCORING STANDARDS

SCORE DESCRIPTION

6 While not reserved for a perfect answer, a grade of 6 demonstrates a full understanding and discussion of the material facts and applicable law, a recognition and discussion of all of the significant issues, and a strong ability to reason to a conclusion.

5 An answer deserving a grade of 5 demonstrates a fairly complete understanding and discussion of the material facts and applicable law, a recognition and discussion of nearly all of the issues, and a clear competence in reasoning to a conclusion.

4 An answer deserving a grade of 4 demonstrates a reasonable understanding and discussion of the material facts and applicable law, a recognition and discussion of most of the issues, and an adequate ability to reason to a conclusion.

3 An answer deserving a grade of 3 demonstrates some competence, but contains an inadequate or incomplete discussion of the material facts or applicable law, fails to some degree to recognize or discuss significant issues, or exhibits inferior reasoning ability.

2 An answer deserving a grade of 2 demonstrates little understanding of the material facts or applicable law, fails to recognize or discuss sufficient or significant issues, exhibits poor reasoning ability, does not adequately respond to the question asked, or contains some combination of these deficiencies.

1 An answer deserving a grade of 1 demonstrates a fundamental deficiency in understanding or recognizing material facts, issues or applicable law, exhibits little or no reasoning ability, or is largely unsupported by reasoning.

0 An answer deserving a grade of 0 is totally deficient or non-responsive.

The target score for each essay is a "4"—but the scores are scaled cumulatively and combined with your scaled MPT and MBE scores. Thus, it is not necessary to get a "4" on every essay in order to pass. On the flip side, it's possible to receive a score of "4" on every essay and still fail the exam if you bomb the MPT and/or MBE.

But as a general rule of thumb, receiving a median MPT and MBE score and a raw essay score of 24 (which would be six essays averaging a "4" on each) equates to a passing score. I won't bore you with the mathematics of "scaling" the various sections, but the number to keep in mind is 410. That is the magic bar exam "passing" number. (So write that number down on the cover of your energy notebook and start visualizing your reality.)

Breaking Down the Essay Portion of the Exam

Day 1 of the exam is the essay day. You will be given three hours to complete six (6) essays in the morning session. Accordingly, you will have 30 minutes to complete each essay. Monitor your time closely—you will not likely start exactly at 9:00 a.m. If you start at 9:11, write your time on the top of your essay and the time when you need to move on to the next essay (in this example, 9:41).

In July of 2011, the Arizona bar exam changed to consist mostly of Multistate Examination questions in the pool of six (6) essay questions. However, the Committee reserved the right to include Arizona essays and examinees should still be sure to apply Arizona law distinctions to every essay question.

The Difference between Bar Exam Essays and Law School Exam Essays

You will notice at first glance that there are similarities between law school exam essays and bar exam essays. After all, you are given a fact pattern and asked to answer a question—sometimes a specific question and sometimes a more open-ended question. And you answer the essays in a similar manner as you did in law school: by noting the relevant issue(s), stating the applicable rules of law, providing a well-reasoned analysis, and, finally, giving a conclusion.

There are, however, important differences between law school essays and bar exam essays. And it is key to your doing well on the bar exam to understand the differences between the two. Essentially, there are three main differences between law school essay exams and bar essays. First, in law school you were generally rewarded with more points for giving both sides to an argument. You were even awarded points when the counter-argument wasn't very good, but was plausible. On bar essays, this is generally not true. It's occasionally true—but for the most part the Examiners want you take a side and give a well-reasoned conclusion.

The second big difference: the "omitted fact" type of essay question in law school does not normally show up on the bar exam. The omitted fact essay is where you haven't been given enough facts to evaluate whether the entire rule has been satisfied. An example of this might be from a contracts exam where John "recently graduated from high school" and signed a contract to buy a car. In this example, the examinee is not given enough facts to know John's exact age (and thus whether he had the capacity to enter into a contract).

The Bar Examiners generally do not do this—they almost always provide you with all of the facts necessary to fully answer the question. Specifically, they give you the relevant facts necessary to analyze all parts of a given rule. An example of this can be seen from the July 2007 Bar Exam, Question #1 (Criminal Law):[6]

> Harry and David earn their living by snatching purses. They drive around wealthy neighborhoods in Scottsdale, Arizona, until they see a well-dressed woman walking alone. One night, after spotting a potential victim ...

In the rest of the fact pattern, it becomes clear that robbery was an issue to be discussed by the examinee. In Arizona, robbery is the taking of personal property of another by force or threat with intent to permanently deprive him of it. In the real world, intent is often difficult to discern or prove. Here, however, the facts make it clear that Harry and David intended to permanently deprive the would-be victim of her purse because they "earn[ed] their living by snatching purses." The bottom line: most every fact you need to analyze an issue is given to you in the fact pattern.

The third big difference between law school essays and bar exam essays is that the Bar Examiners usually do not give irrelevant or red herring facts. Once in a while they will, but not normally. And as we all know, the warped and demented minds of law school professors love to include red herrings and irrelevant facts in their essay exams. As such, most every fact matters on the bar exam. Below are a few examples. The first one is from the February 2007 Bar Exam, Question #3 (Wills):

> Adrian, a man suffering from OCD (obsessive compulsive disorder), became fixated on his own mortality to such an extent that he decided to visit with an

---

6. The portions of the Arizona essay questions in this book are reprinted under licensing agreement with and permission of the Arizona Supreme Court, Administrative Office of the Courts. No part of any question may be reproduced or transmitted in any form unless expressly permitted in writing by the Arizona Supreme Court. The author greatly thanks the Court for the licensing agreement and permission to reprint selected essay passages.

> attorney to get his affairs in order. He hired a duly licensed Arizona attorney, Perry, who spent the next four years preparing Adrian's will.

After the initial paragraph, the following seven paragraphs contain many details and facts about Adrian's will and various actions he takes. Thus, it would be easy to overlook the very first fact—the fact that Adrian suffers from OCD. Why did the bar examiners include this fact? Answer: because they wanted the examinee to address the issue of capacity. (Note that in this case, Adrian's OCD wouldn't likely invalidate the will, but it is your responsibility to tell the grader that you know this, given that they included this fact.) Most every fact matters, and issues come from facts. Here's a similar example from the same exam—February 2007, Question #2 (Contracts):

> December 2, 2006 was a very busy day for Kevin, the owner of Kevin's Acting Supplies, a business with two locations in Tucson, Arizona and Phoenix, Arizona. It all started after a fitful night's sleep brought about by an overindulgence of intoxicating beverages and recreational pharmaceuticals. Keith woke up and as the haze started to clear, he realized that he had forgotten that today was the birthday of Britney, his girlfriend, and he had neglected to purchase a present.

Again, many facts follow these opening sentences—including potential contract formations between Kevin and five different people. It would be easy to overlook the seemingly irrelevant fact(s) in the second sentence, but not if you are paying attention to every single fact. Even though voluntary impairment isn't a defense to a contract formation, the facts still raise the issue and it's your responsibility to tell the grader that, while the intoxication is an "issue," it is not one that will invalidate an otherwise valid contract because Kevin's intoxication was voluntary. Little things such as this can sometimes be the difference between a score of "3" and a score of "4."

Because all issues come from facts, take note of every single fact—it's usually there for a reason. If you find yourself having trouble spotting issues on practice exams, really bring your focus onto every single fact given. Issues are always born from facts.

Guidelines for Writing Great Essays

Generally speaking, answer the questions in the order you get them. You don't want to waste time sifting through the questions to answer the subject you know "best." There is one exception to this rule: if there is a subject that triggers anxiety or a mental block, you might want to consider moving that subject to the end when it comes up. It's important to start off with a positive first step, so if you are absolutely hung up on constitutional law, consider saving it until the end. Moreover, if you do run out of time, it's better to run out of time on a subject that you don't know very well.

You should ***not***, however, sift through each essay and try to rank the questions in a particular order; nor should you try to search out a particular subject in order to answer it first (or last). Doing so will cost you valuable time, and you will need all the time you can get. Answer the questions in order, and if/when you come across the subject you loathe—or don't know very well—feel free to put that essay off until the end.

Read the Call of the Question First

One of the most important pieces of advice for doing well on an essay: read the call of the question first. The "call" of the question is the part that "calls" for you to answer a specific (or general) question. The call is almost always located in the last paragraph of the fact pattern (and often in the last sentence). The call of the question is the most important part of essay writing—because you will be asked something specific here and you need to respond specifically.

Moreover, if you read the call of the question FIRST, you will be grounded in the subject matter. This will put you in a "torts frame of mind" (if, of course, it's a torts question) and give better context to the fact pattern. This is important because you may not know UNTIL the call of the question what the actual subject is—a torts question could look like a property question, which could look like a contracts question, which could look like a corporations question, and so forth and so on.

Below are a few examples of opening fact pattern paragraphs. See if you can recognize the subject being tested. The first one is from the February 2008 Bar Exam, Question #7:

> Ever since childhood, Harry had a tremendous interest in and affinity for the art of magic. He started performing at school events and continued to develop and work on his act all the way through college. After graduating from college and marrying Elvira, Harry took his magic act on the road. Traveling from town to town became especially difficult after the birth of their daughter, Doris, and Harry decided to settle down and concentrate on his "day job."
>
> Despite being content with his lot in life, Harry always wanted to return to the stage. A few months ago, he learned of an illusionist competition called *American Magician*. He decided to enter and polished up one of his favorite tricks, Russian Roulette. He uses six revolvers and has an audience member place a bullet in one of the guns at random while he is blindfolded. Then, with increasing dramatic flair, he places each gun to his head and pulls the trigger until only one gun (the gun with the bullet) remains. Although this illusion appears extremely dangerous, it is actual [sic] quite safe if one knows how it is done.

Okay, we're two lengthy paragraphs into the fact pattern and there is still no indication as to what subject we're dealing with. Community property may have jumped into your mind due to the marriage and birth of a child (as well as the game show competition, which has been fodder for past community property questions). You could also be thinking criminal law or torts, due to the fact that guns are present and being fired in the midst of audience members.

If, however, you read the call of the question first, the subject at issue is more than obvious. The first three words of the call of the question (the last paragraph) states as follows: "Is Harry's will valid?" Knowing you are dealing with a wills question will help give you the needed context for digesting the lengthy first two paragraphs in the fact pattern.

Below are a few other examples. The first is from the February 2004 Bar Exam, Question #9:

> You and your spouse are having dinner at the home of Susan Swensen, president of Sweets Corp. ("Sweets"). Sweets, which is one of your biggest clients, is in the business of operating retail sweets shops in shopping malls. While Mr. Swensen, Susan's husband, is passing around dessert, Susan says, "That reminds me," and begins to tell about a plan that she has just hatched.
>
> Susan intends to enter into a contract with Patrick Pete, owner of 51% of the outstanding shares of Pete's Treats, Inc. ("Pete's Treats"). Pete's Treats, the largest competitor of Sweets, is owned by a total of eight shareholders.

Again, we're two paragraphs into the fact pattern and there is still no indication as to what subject we're dealing with. At first, you see the words "you and your spouse," which might lead you into thinking community property may be on the horizon. Then you see words such as "Corp." and "51% of the outstanding shares of Pete's Treats, Inc.," causing you to anticipate a corporations question. And of course, anytime you see something about a "plan" being "hatched" you most likely think about criminal law. Finally, the first sentence of paragraph #2 invokes contracts with the "intends to enter into a contract" language.

So which subject is being tested? Answer: none of them. The question is actually a professional responsibility question. This, of course, is made perfectly clear by the call of the question, which starts off with the words, "[p]lease discuss the legal and professional responsibility issues raised by Susan's plan...."

Here's another example. This one is from the February 2007 Bar Exam, Question #9:

> Our story begins in 2000 when Richard and his buddy, Steve, graduated from law school and were living the good life as bachelors in Miami, Florida. Being fed up with his legal job, Richard turned his attention to his true passion, computers. During their spare time, Richard and Steve designed a website called YouScreen where registered users could post video or audio recordings of whatever they wanted. They incorporated the business with Richard and Steve each owning 50% of the stock. What started out as a quirky website, quickly turned into a "hot property." In the same fashion, so did Richard and soon he had a girlfriend named Lauren.
>
> In early 2003, Lauren's mother died with a valid will devising to her a beautiful home situated on 100 acres in Flagstaff, Arizona. Because the house was fully paid for, and there was no mortgage, Lauren and Richard decided to move there and live together. Richard resigned his employment with YouScreen, but kept his 50% of the company's stock. Richard then moved to Arizona, and took the Arizona bar exam. He passed the exam, and went on to develop a significant intellectual property practice.

Do you know what subject is being tested yet? At first, you might have thought this was a corporations question, given the references to incorporation of a business and the stock percentages. Or, because lawyers are involved, perhaps professional responsibility came to mind. Did the references to "hot property" or "100 acres" make you think that this was a property question? And, of course, the reference to a "valid will" may have made you think that this was a wills question.

If, however, you had read the call of the question first, you would immediately know that community property was the subject being tested. Here is the call of the question: "The hearing on the divorce is tomorrow. To assist the judge in determining which property to award to Richard and Lauren and liabilities each party must assume, fully discuss all of the issues raised by these facts in an organized manner applying applicable Arizona law."

Here's the last example—from the July 2005 Bar Exam, Question #7:

> Lucinda Lawyer was walking to work one morning in downtown Phoenix when she witnessed an accident involving a delivery van and a cyclist. Because she recognized the cyclist as Armando, her accountant, she rushed over to see if he was hurt. He appeared to have some broken bones, so she called 911 and reassured him until the ambulance arrived to care for Armando and the police arrived to question the driver of the other vehicle.
>
> A week later, Lucinda called Armando at his office to see how he was doing. When the receptionist informed her that he was still at HealthCorp Hospital, Lucinda called him there to wish him well. In the course of their conversation, Lucinda asked what had happened. "This guy just came out of nowhere and hit me. He was driving a delivery truck for Express Package Service, but he told the cops he was off duty. This is a real disaster, because you know I'm in practice for myself and its tax time, so I'm losing a ton of business."

Given Armando's injury (and the bystander coming to his aid), this would appear to be a torts question. However, references to Armando's business at the end of paragraph two may have made you think about corporations. Again, reading the call of the question first makes the subject obvious. Here it is: "Please discuss Lucinda's obligations under the Arizona Rules of Professional Conduct and whether she complied with them."

As you can see, reading the call of the question helps ground you in the subject matter. Facts take on different meanings depending on the subject being tested, so it's key to know the context of those facts (e.g., what subject is being tested) as you begin reading.

Moreover, it's important to remember that, most of the time, when you write out practice essays, you will know the subject matter before you begin. As such, it's important to replicate your practice by knowing each subject before reading the facts on the actual exam. So—read the call of the question first!

After Reading the Call of the Question ...

After you read the call of the question, read the fact pattern with the call in mind. Digest the facts and look for issues. If you are comfortable doing so, jot down issues in the margins. Read slowly, read carefully, and read critically. Keep in mind that (1) most every fact matters, and (2) issues always come from facts. I recommend reading the fact pattern twice. At the end, be sure to read the call of the question a second time. It is absolutely crucial to answer the specific question asked (rather than giving a "brain dump" of everything you know about a particular topic).

At this point, I am often asked—should I outline or should I just start writing? Like any good answer to a good law school question, the answer is: IT DEPENDS. If you become adept at jotting down issues or other notes as you read the facts, this could replace your "outline," for each question. Outlining your answer ahead of time also depends on how comfortable you feel with the time constraints. You should know this if you've done enough practice essays—are you usually short on time? If so, outlining might not be the best thing for you.

On the flip side, if you outline before you write, you are much less likely to skip over or forget a major issue—so long as you remember to refer back to your outline before you move on to the next question. In my experience with tutoring, sometimes I will see the examinee's scratch paper that has a key issue noted in the "outline" but the answer fails to note the issue. As such, remember that you don't get any points for your outline—only what you have written down or typed on your answer sheet counts.

In sum, outlining is never a bad idea, as long as it is quick and doesn't distract you. Noting the issues in the margins while reading the fact pattern may be just as effective for some of you. Practice both, and you should have a good idea as to which approach is best for you.

Writing the Essay

You have six hours to write twelve essays—not a lot of time. Keep it simple. Know exactly how you are going to attack your essay answers. Whenever possible, plug into a template for each topic. Below are some bullet points to keep in mind when answering essays, all of which I will discuss in more detail later. But for now, I think it's important to look at the big picture before dissecting each part.

1) Have an organizational framework for writing your answers
   - Usually, an IRAC or CRAC (conclusion first) is a decent starting place for your macro-organization for a bar essay exam.
   - Whatever writing template you use, be consistent, and be comfortable with it.
   - Try to plug into a format that will maximize your point value and force you to apply facts to law.
2) Be precise and be concise
   - You don't have time to write any other way.
   - And, to be honest, you don't want to—be specific and get to the point to be most effective on a bar exam or in the real world.
   - Answer the specific question asked.
3) Make your essay look professional and easily readable
   - First, use headings for your issues to guide the reader.

- Use transitions whenever you can.
- Examples: Also, Furthermore, Moreover, Although, Conversely, Moreover, Therefore, etc. And don't be afraid to use the generic, "First ... Second ... Next ..." transitions.
- The easier you make it on the grader to understand and follow, the better off you will be.

4) Keep track of your time
   - You don't want to spend an inordinate amount of time on any one essay.
   - As a general rule, stick to the time allotted for each question as closely as you can.
   - Write down when you start each essay so you don't lose track of time.
5) After you are done with a question, LET IT GO
   - Thinking about how poorly (or how well) you did on a previous essay will only detract from your focus. DO NOT LET THIS HAPPEN.
   - Know that there will likely be an essay question or two that throws you, do your best, and move on.

Poor Essay Scores

1. A Law Problem

Generally speaking, a low score on an essay can be attributed to one of two things: (1) a law problem ... or (2) a writing problem. Simply put, a "law problem" means you do not know the law. If you don't know the law, you cannot pass the bar exam. It's as simple as that. There is no "faking it" on a bar exam essay. You cannot go into the test knowing "most" of the law—know everything that is going to be covered and know each "rule" by heart.

You cannot have a "general" idea of the rule of law—analysis is the art of applying specific facts to specific rules to see whether each part of the rule has been met by these particular facts. Good examinees (and good lawyers) are detail oriented. That, above all else, is true. Right? (Well, that depends on what your definition of "is" ... is.) So ... know the law backwards and forwards. And, of course, know every exception, extension, and explanation necessary to communicate your analysis effectively. (For more on study techniques for remembering the law, refer to Chapter 2.)

2. A Writing Problem

Contrary to what you may believe, you can know every aspect of every rule of law, and still do poorly on the bar exam. Passing most often depends on not only knowing the law, but also knowing how to take the bar exam. This is where the "writing problem" comes into play.

Many of my tutorees who have failed the bar often tell me that they studied twelve hours a day and knew every single rule of law (and thus couldn't believe they failed). And, in fact, this is often the case. Many of them truly did know most all of the law that was tested, but they didn't put their analyses down on paper in a way that maximized their points.

What I refer to as a "writing problem" falls into two main categories: (1) an overall organization problem, and (2) an organizational analysis problem. I'll break down each, starting with the former.

A. *An Overall Organization Problem*

You want to make your grader "happy" when grading—and "happy" equates to having good overall organization that is easy to follow. If you are all over the place and scattered, you are likely not going to do well on your essays. If you give your analysis before stating the applicable rule or the issue that you are attempting to address, it is going to be more difficult to digest what you are trying to communicate.

Thus, for your overall (or "macro") organization, some form of IRAC (Issue, Rule, Analysis, Conclusion), CRAC (Conclusion, Rule, Analysis, Conclusion), or CREAC (Conclusion, Rule, Explanation of the Rule, Analysis, Conclusion) will work well. This is especially true when dealing with the time pressures of the bar exam.

Whatever acronym you put on it, you want an overall (macro) organization that gives the issue (or conclusion) up front, states the rule for that issue, applies the facts to the rule governing the issue, and gives a conclusion. Personally, I am a fan of "IRAC" for a couple of reasons.

First, it's easier to state the issue (by simply underlining "Negligence" in a heading), as opposed to writing out a full-blown conclusion ("John was likely guilty of negligence") when you begin your answer. Furthermore, you will often not know your conclusion at the outset of your answer. Many times, you will need to reason through your analysis (fact application to the rule of law) before you can make an educated guess as to the conclusion. Finally, you will want to state your conclusion at the end of your answer. Stating the conclusion at the beginning and the end will waste time.

The IRAC framework may be oversimplified for the practice of law (or even, some would argue, for a law school exam), but on the time-pressured bar exam, IRAC works well. Other organizational frameworks can be just as effective, but you cannot go wrong with IRAC as your starting point for organizing your essay answer.

As long as we're talking about overall organization, let me add another organizational tip when a question involves multiple parties. When multiple players are involved and you are asked to discuss the civil liability or criminal liability of each, organize your answer around the people, not the crimes or theories of liability. Thus, if you are asked to discuss all crimes A and B may have committed, address all crimes for A first, then B. This is true even if both A and B may have committed a few of the same crimes.

B. An Organizational Analysis Problem

The biggest mistake examinees make in writing is within their analyses. We all know that "analysis" is supposed to be applying facts to rules. This is certainly true—but I am amazed at how many people do this incorrectly. (By "incorrectly" I mean writing in a way that fails to maximize their score.) Knowing how to analyze the law vis-à-vis a fact pattern (often referred to as "logical reasoning" or "application") is something most every law school graduate knows how to do. But writing that analysis down on paper is often problematic on the time-pressured bar exam.

What makes for a well-written analysis? Answer: **matching up specific facts to specific parts of the rule.** Now let's step back for a minute and think about this—because this is what attorneys really do. Attorneys argue that the facts of the case have satisfied all parts of the relevant rule of law. Fact A satisfies the first part, Fact B satisfies the second part, and Facts C, D, and E satisfy the third part. Thus, each part of the rule has been met by the facts and my client wins. Essentially, that is what you do as an attorney.

The organizational analysis—the "A" of IRAC—is the most important part of your writing, and often the most overlooked. The "A" in analysis can also be referred to as a "micro-format"—as opposed to the big picture "macro-format."

So let's look at a typical fact pattern and how to write a good essay answer. This is a somewhat typical fact pattern that you might see on an essay exam. Read over the fact pattern carefully (but don't forget what you've already learned—read the call of the question first to ground yourself in the subject matter).

Example 4-1

Sample Fact Pattern—Criminal Law Essay

> Sam was a petty thief who needed a big score. He heard that Old Man Bill Johnson had just purchased a $10,000 painting, which Sam thought he could easily sell to his art collector cousin. So Sam spent weeks staking out the Johnson house, "casing it" for the perfect crime. When Sam had the household routine down cold, he put his elaborate plan into action. One day, after Mr. Johnson left for work, Sam drove his car from down the street and parked in front of the Johnson house—which was no easy task because Sam had been drinking for several hours. Sam then ran to the Johnsons'

> front door, kicked in the door, ran into the living room, and grabbed the $10,000 painting off of the wall.
>
> As Sam ran out of the house, he was startled to see Mr. Johnson standing in front of him in the driveway. Both men froze, but then Sam decided to make the best of the situation. "I need some meal money, pops," Sam yelled. "Give me your wallet or I'll bash your head in!" Mr. Johnson pulled out his cell phone and frantically started to dial. Sam kicked Mr. Johnson in the stomach, then pushed him to the ground. As Mr. Johnson wallowed on the ground in pain, Sam rifled through the elderly man's pants pockets. When Sam found the old man's wallet, he grabbed it, grabbed the painting and took off running. Old Man Bill Johnson suffered internal bleeding, and later died in surgery due to surgeon error.
>
> Discuss and evaluate all crimes Sam may have committed, including any defenses.

If you read the call of the question first, you would immediately know that this was a criminal law essay. Hopefully, a few of the big issues jumped out at you right away. Let's discuss two of the big ones and look at some sample answers.

Burglary and robbery were two of the big issues that might have jumped out at you as you read the fact pattern. Here are the Arizona rules for both of those crimes:

> **Burglary**: Breaking and entering into the dwelling of another with intent to commit a felony therein.
>
> **Robbery**: Taking of property from the person of another by force or threat with intent to permanently deprive him of the property.

Keeping in mind the need for good fact application, take a look at the following sample answers for these two issues. Please note that the "model" answer is only a partial answer. There would certainly be other "issues" to address, but we are only going to discuss the issues of burglary and robbery.

Example 4-2

Partial "Model" Answer—Criminal Law Essay

<u>The first issue is, did the Defendant commit burglary?</u>

Burglary is defined as "breaking and entering into a dwelling of another with intent to commit a felony therein." Based on the facts given to us, Sam needed a big "score" so he kicked down the door of the Johnson house, walked inside and stole the $10,000 painting. As such, Sam is guilty of the crime of burglary.

<u>The second issue is, did the Defendant commit robbery?</u>

Robbery is defined as the "taking of property from the person of another by force or intimidation with intent to deprive him of it permanently." In the case at bar, after Sam left the house, he saw Mr. Johnson in front of him and yelled, "give me your wallet or I'll bash your head in." He then kicked Mr. Johnson in the stomach, pushed him to the ground, seized his wallet, and ran off with it. Thus, Sam has satisfied all of the elements of robbery and will be guilty of robbery.

So let's discuss the partial answer, starting with the burglary issue. Clearly, burglary is an issue—which is noted by the heading. The answer then identifies the correct rule with specificity. The answer then gives all of the relevant facts and a specific (and correct) conclusion. Perfect answer, right?

Not exactly. What's wrong with the answer? The IRAC format is followed perfectly, right? The issue is correctly identified, right? The correct rule is given, right? The answer then notes all of the relevant facts that bear on the relevant elements of burglary, right?

The last question is the relevant one. Yes, the answer does "note" all of the relevant facts, but there is no application, no actual analysis in the answer. The answer merely recites facts, which you never want to do. You want to link up relevant facts with relevant parts of the rule. Stating the issue, stating the rule, listing facts, and coming up with the conclusion is a format many students "think" provides analysis, but it does not. Analysis is APPLYING facts to rules; reciting facts is not the same as applying facts.

Many students go through the analysis in their head without correctly noting it on paper. Even though you think something is obvious, you have to state the obvious to maximize your score. This is where the "organizational analysis" format comes into play. And I'll tell you how to be more effective at that in just a second. But first, let's take a look at the robbery answer, reprinted below:

> The second issue is, did the Defendant commit robbery?
>
> Robbery is defined as the "taking of property from the person of another by force or intimidation with intent to deprive him of it permanently." In the case at bar, after Sam left the house, he saw Mr. Johnson in front of him and yelled, "give me your wallet or I'll bash your head in." He then kicked Mr. Johnson in the stomach, pushed him to the ground, seized his wallet, and ran off with it. Thus, Sam has satisfied all of the elements of robbery and will be guilty of robbery.

This answer has the same blueprint as the burglary answer, correct? At first glance, this seems like a very good answer—but, again, there is no actual analysis here. The writer is most likely going through the analysis in her head, but that is not what shows up on paper. And the grader can only give points for what is on paper.

So—how do we do a better job at giving our analysis or our "application"? In essence, show all of your work. Think of this like 8th grade math. Sometimes, things seem too obvious to note, but you have to show all of your work to maximize your point potential. Even if it's obvious from the facts that a particular element or part of the rule is met, state which specific fact (or facts) make it so. Don't recite facts, integrate facts—this is analysis. SHOW ALL OF YOUR WORK.

To ensure you are matching up facts and rules (and to increase your efficiency), I suggest the following template for your analysis/ application/micro-format: the "Here ... because" blueprint of essay writing. When it's time for the analysis (after you have identified the issue and given the applicable rule) the first word you should write is "HERE." (Of course, you could write, "in the case at bar" or something similar, but "here" takes up less time and energy, while still signaling to the grader that you are moving into your analysis.)

The rest of micro-format goes like this: "Here (element/part of the rule) is/isn't met because of Fact Y. Also, part #2 of the rule is/isn't met because of Fact Y. Furthermore, part 3 of the rule is/isn't met because of Fact Z. Thus, the rule is/is not satisfied."

This format ensures you are tying facts to rules. Note that after the first "here" you will probably want to write "also" or "furthermore" for the following sentences. If a subsequent part of the rule is *not* supported by the facts, you would likely want to write "however" or "conversely."

Examples 4-3 and 4-4 illustrate this format for an evidence/hearsay/dying declaration analysis. The "rule" for this hearsay exception states that such a statement is admissible if the speaker (or "declarant") believed his death was imminent and the statement concerned the cause of what he believed to be his impending death.

Example 4-3

> Here, the declarant believed his death was imminent because he said, "I'm not going to make it." Also, the statement concerned the cause of his death because he said, "Tom's the one who did this to me." Thus, the statement will be admissible as a dying declaration hearsay exception.

Example 4-4

> Here, the declarant believed his death was imminent because he said, "I'm not going to make it." However, the statement did not concern the cause of his death because his statement, "Tom has always hated me" didn't deal with being stabbed. Thus, the statement will not be admissible as a dying declaration hearsay exception.

Note in Examples 4-3 and 4-4 how each part of the rule is proven or negated by a specific fact. The facts are integrated—not merely recited. The word "because" is an analysis word (a "causal connector") that should appear throughout each answer. It's also a good idea to quote specific statements whenever possible (especially when a statement is critical to the analysis).

As a general rule of thumb, break the rule into its separate parts. If there are two parts of the rule, there needs to be (at least) two sentences of application, and then a conclusion sentence. The format literally forces you to apply facts to parts of the rule, rather than recite facts and go through the analysis in your head. Here again is a skeletal template without reference to a specific situation. (Assume there would be three parts to the rule.)

Here (element/rule part 1) is met because (fact A). Also, (element/rule part 2) is met because (fact B). Finally, (element/rule part 3) is met because (fact C). Thus, (the rule is satisfied).

Given our new format, how would we re-write our criminal essay dealing with Sam, Mr. Johnson, and the issues of burglary and robbery? At this point, if you really want to get the most out of this book, take a few minutes and try to write out an answer for both issues. Remember—practice is the key to doing well, and there is never any time better than the present moment. Refer back to page 36 for the applicable rules of law.

Before we look at a model answer, I'd like to throw out this disclaimer: there are a number of ways that you can write out an answer to our issues and get the full point value. The format I am suggesting is one that forces you to apply/analyze, and it should increase your overall efficiency. Thus, it works well, but other "blueprints" could work, too. Okay ... let's look at these answers, starting with burglary. I have given the "old" answer and the "new" answer together for a basis of comparison.

Example 4-5

The "Old" Burglary Answer

> The first issue is, did the Defendant commit burglary?
>
> Burglary is defined as "breaking and entering into a dwelling of another with intent to commit a felony therein." Based on the facts given to us, Sam needed a big "score" so he kicked down the door of the Johnson house, walked inside and stole the $10,000 painting. As such, Sam is guilty of the crime of burglary.

The "New" Burglary Answer

> Burglary
>
> Burglary is defined as "breaking and entering into a dwelling of another with intent to commit a theft or felony therein." Here, Sam committed breaking and entering because he kicked down the door and entered the house. Also, it was a dwelling of another because Mr. Johnson lived there. Furthermore, Sam had the requisite intent to commit theft because he had been "casing the place" for weeks and was going to "sell" the painting to his art collector cousin. Finally, he committed theft because he took Mr. Johnson's $10,000 painting from inside the house. Thus, Sam is guilty of burglary.

The first difference you will notice—you do not have to write out, "The issue is whether D is guilty of burglary" or whatever crime you are discussing. It's sufficient just to give the issue its own heading, as I've done here. Every little bit of time you save might come into play on the last essay.

Of course, after noting the issue you are discussing, the applicable rule needs to be the first thing you write down. And in our example, it is. There are no wasted words to introduce it—it just states the applicable rule with specificity.

Utilizing the "here ... because" model you see what we get in our "new" answer. Note how each part of the rule is matched up with a specific fact or facts that prove to the grader exactly how and why each part of the rule is met. You can see how this microformat forces you to address each part of the rule—which is exactly what you have to do if you want to do well on the essay portion of the bar exam. Also note how the question provides all of the facts you need to match up to all parts of the rule. Now let's take a look at the two "robbery" answers—the "old" one and the "new" one.

Example 4-6

The "Old" Robbery Answer

> <u>The second issue is, did the Defendant commit robbery?</u>
>
> Robbery is defined as the "taking of property from the person of another by force or intimidation with intent to deprive him of it permanently." In the case at bar, after Sam left the house, he saw Mr. Johnson in front of him and yelled, "give me your wallet or I'll bash your head in." He then kicked Mr. Johnson in the stomach, pushed him to the ground, seized his wallet, and ran off with it. Thus, Sam has satisfied all of the elements of robbery and will be guilty of robbery.

The "New" Robbery Answer

> <u>Robbery</u>
>
> Robbery is the taking of property from the person of another by force or intimidation with intent to deprive him of it permanently. Here, Sam took property from the person of Mr. Johnson because Sam rifled through the victim's pockets and took his wallet. Also,

> he did so by force because he kicked the victim in the stomach and pushed him to the ground. Finally, he did so with intent to permanently deprive the victim of his wallet, as evidenced by him saying, "I need meal money." Thus, Sam satisfies all of the elements of robbery and will be guilty of robbery.

Note again how the "old" answer does indeed list the relevant facts. The facts, however, are merely listed and not integrated into an analysis. Here's a rule of thumb: never list a fact unless it is within a sentence that proves or negates part of the rule.

Also note in the "new" answer I switched up the "because" with "as evidenced by" in the fourth sentence. As you get more comfortable with the format, you might substitute different words for a better read, but "because" will work perfectly well as your "analysis connector" most every time.

Just to make sure you feel comfortable with this format, here's another example of a "fact application" from a criminal procedure question (a *Miranda* issue). The facts are from the February 2004 Bar Exam (Question #2). As a refresher, *Miranda* rights are required whenever a person is in "custodial interrogation."

Example 4-7

> In the facts at bar, the Officer put Abe in handcuffs and then threw him into the back seat of the squad car. Also, the Officer rigorously questioned Abe about his involvement in an illegal drug ring in the area. As such, Abe was likely in custodial interrogation and should have been read his *Miranda* rights.

Example 4-8

> Here, Abe was likely in "custody" because the Officer put him in handcuffs and threw him into the backseat of the squad car. Also, the Officer interrogated Abe because he "rigorously questioned" him about his "in-

> volvement in an illegal drug ring" in the area. Thus, custodial interrogation took place and Abe should have been read his *Miranda* rights.

The two examples are further illustrations of a poorly written application and a well-written application. Again, the first example merely lists facts and draws a conclusion without "showing all of the work." The second example (Example 4-8) ties specific facts to elements of the rule, and it's clearly better.

Below is another example from torts. Assume the "rule" for defamation is as follows: defamatory language of or concerning the Plaintiff, publication to a third person, and damage to the Plaintiff's reputation.

Example 4-9

> Defamation
>
> Defamation is actionable when there is defamatory language that is of or concerning the Plaintiff, publication to a third party, and damage to the Plaintiff's reputation.
>
> Here Defendant used defamatory language that concerned Plaintiff because he called the Plaintiff a "criminal and an adulterer." Also, the information was published to a third party because Defendant made the comment at an office meeting with ten people present. Finally, the statement caused damage to the Plaintiff's reputation because he was shunned by many staff members and later fired.

At this point, some of you might be thinking—this is far too simplistic for a bar exam analysis. Au contraire, mon frère. Simple is profound. You want to keep it simple because you are going to be in a serious time crunch. Moreover, you want to keep it simple because that usually makes for a better read—one that will make your grader happy. The graders have their grading rubric of rules and points of analyses that they are looking for, and the easier you make it for them to read, the better your score is going to be.

Finally, you have a very challenging task ahead of you. You have a LOT of law to learn in a relatively short amount of time. You want to go into the exam with a specific plan as to how you are going to write your essays. With practice, your format or "template" should be second-nature to you. It doesn't have to be the format I am suggesting, but it needs to be a format where you are integrating fact and law in your writing.

Admittedly, this format works better for some subjects than others. But regardless of the subject, you still have different parts of rules—and you need to analyze each part of the rule by applying specific facts from the fact pattern.

5

What Type of Essay Writer Are You?

As I mentioned in Chapter 1, knowing yourself will take you a long way toward passing the bar exam. Accordingly, it's important to know what kind of essay writer you are. Take a look at the examples below. These are the three most common ways examinees answer questions on the bar—but only one of them will maximize your score. Recognizing different types of answers will help you avoid falling into similar patterns that undermine your essay scores.

For this exercise, assume the definition for first-degree murder is "the unlawful killing of another with malice aforethought and causation." I've given a fact pattern that is merely one small part of an overall question, as indicated by the "partial" portion of the facts. As such, the answers below the facts are partial as well. See if you can pick out the "best" answer of the three (and at this point I hope you can).

Example 5-1

Partial Fact Pattern—Criminal Law Essay

Bob is showing off his new gun to Ted. Thinking there are no bullets in the gun, Bob reenacts a scene from his favorite movie—points the gun at Ted and pulls the trigger, hitting and killing Ted. With what crimes can Bob be convicted? Please evaluate fully, including any and all defenses that may apply.

ANSWER #1 (PARTIAL)

First-degree murder

First-degree murder is the intentional killing of another with malice aforethought and causation. One acts with malice aforethought when he acts knowingly and purposefully. Here, although Bob was the actual and proximate cause of Ted's death, he had no malice aforethought (e.g., he didn't act knowingly and/or purposefully). Thus, he cannot be guilty of first-degree murder.

ANSWER #2 (PARTIAL)

First-degree murder

First-degree murder is the intentional killing of another with malice aforethought and causation. One acts with malice aforethought when he acts knowingly and purposefully. Here, Bob was only "showing off his new gun to Ted." When reenacting a scene from his favorite movie, Bob pointed the gun at Ted and pulled the trigger, killing Ted. However, Bob did not think there were any bullets in the gun. Therefore, Bob cannot be guilty of first-degree murder.

ANSWER #3 (PARTIAL)

First-degree murder

First-degree murder is the intentional killing of another with malice aforethought (acting knowingly and purposefully) and causation. Here, Bob killed another because Ted died. Also, Bob satisfies the causation requirement because but for his act of pointing the gun at Ted and pulling the trigger, Ted would not have died. However, Bob did not act with malice aforethought (did not act knowingly and/or purposefully) because he did not think there were any bullets in the gun. Thus, Bob had no intent to kill Ted and cannot be guilty of first-degree murder.

Okay—these answers are the types that I typically see from examinees. Can you identify which category of writer you fall into? Let's discuss all three answers and figure out which is the better model.

ANSWER #1: The Law-Based Answer

Upon first reading, #1 seems to be on target, right? It first lays out the correct rule of law, and appears at first glance to analyze various parts of the rule, then correctly concludes. But when we look more closely, we can see the flaws.

This answer represents what I call the "law-based" answer. This type of answer gives the rule of law, and then makes a conclusion about the various parts of the rule (elements or factors) without giving specific facts to support those conclusions.

Specifically, what we have in Answer #1 is a conclusion about one of the elements, another conclusion about another element, and then a final conclusion—none of which are supported by any FACTS. Thus, in actuality, the answer is completely devoid of analysis. There can be no analysis without the application of specific facts to specific parts of the rule!

This is a classic example (and mistake) of not showing all of your work. The writer is clearly going through all the steps in his/her head, but it doesn't show on paper. To the grader, the writer could just as easily be guessing at each conclusion. Accordingly, your score is not going to be as high as it could be—despite reaching the correct conclusion. (In this regard, the bar exam parallels a law school essay exam.)

As an aside, you'll notice that Answer #1 has two sentences for the "Rule" portion of the essay. If there are terms that need to be defined in the broader rule, then define them. Here, malice aforethought is one of those terms, and if you want to save time, you can do so with a parenthetical definition after the term (as is indicated in Answer #3).

ANSWER #2: The Fact-Based Answer

This answer is what I call the "fact-based" answer. Again, at first blush, the answer may appear to be a good one. The issue is given, the rule is given, and then the relevant facts are noted. As in Answer #1, this answer also concludes correctly.

However, the answer has no specific factual application to any part of the rule. This is not analysis either. Despite noting the material facts upon which the issue turns, there is no integration of fact and law (which equals "analysis"). I believe I have said it before but I will say it again: THERE CAN BE NO ANALYSIS WITHOUT AN APPLICATION OF FACT TO LAW.

ANSWER #3: The Integrated Answer

Answer #3 is a much better answer. As a disclaimer, I will note again that there are many answers that could be written differently and still get full point value. All I am saying is that Answer #3 is far better than numbers 1 and 2 because it actually gives an analysis. This is what the Bar Examiners want—the ability to discern which facts meet or negate each element of the rule.

Answer #3 is an example of an answer that SHOWS ALL OF THE WORK. It lays out all of the steps that the examinee went through in his/her head. Remember—you have to put it down on paper to maximize your points.

Though #3 is slightly longer than the other two, you will ultimately save time by writing in this template because you will know exactly what you are looking for and exactly how to put it down on paper. (The more you practice, the more efficient you will become.) And, most importantly, the integrated answer will maximize your score.

Because the analysis is such a vital part of doing well on the bar exam, I want to give a few more examples before we move on. They are both examples from the February 2008 Bar Exam. I have only listed the relevant portions of the fact pattern for each.

The first question is from evidence. One of the sub-issues dealt with the dying declaration exception to the hearsay rule. The rule for dying declaration is as follows:

> A statement made by a now unavailable declarant is admissible if:
> (1) the declarant believed her death was imminent, and
> (2) the statement concerned the cause of what she believed to be her impending death.

Here is the relevant portion of the fact pattern (February 2008 Bar Exam, Question #10):

> During its case-in-chief, the prosecution offers an audio recording of a phone call to a police operator. The voice on the recording calmly states, "This is Betty. My husband just stabbed me. He told me last night that he murdered his business partner. Now he has killed me because I know too much." [Betty was later found unconscious, and was in a coma at the time of trial.]

You now have the relevant rule and the relevant facts required to answer this question. Take about five minutes (that's all it should take) and write out an answer. This is part of reinforcing the learning process (active learning). So fight the urge to forgo this step, and write out a quick answer. Come on—it's only five minutes, and it's a step on the road to passing the bar exam. (S/he who takes short cuts will have more difficulty following the path to passing.) After you are done, go to the next page and take a look at the answer(s).

Example 5-2 (ANSWER #1 to Dying Declaration)

> Dying declaration
>
> A statement made by a now unavailable declarant is admissible if: (1) the declarant believed her death was imminent (but need not actually die), and (2) the statement concerned the cause of what she believed to be her impending death. The reason for the rule is because it is thought that people on their death beds are not likely to tell lies.
>
> Here, Betty is unavailable to testify at trial. Also, she made the relevant statement while truly believing her death was imminent. Also, the statement specifically concerned the cause of her death. Thus, all elements are met and Betty's statements will be admissible under the dying declaration hearsay exception.

How does your answer match up with this one? Hopefully, your answer isn't very similar. Again, the answer above is one with a "false analysis"—one devoid of fact application. Although changed slightly, this answer is from an actual student I tutored. It was clear that she knew the analysis—but again, failed to show all of her work.

One other important point—take note of the last sentence in the "rule" paragraph in Answer #1: "The reason for the rule is because it is thought that people on their death beds are not likely to tell lies." While this is true, it is superfluous and a great example of a time waster. The Bar Examiners do not want to know all of the arcane or esoteric information you know about a particular issue/topic. Your job is to answer the specific question asked by noting issues, giving applicable rules, applying facts to rules, and concluding. Period. Your job is difficult enough without adding superfluous verbiage.

Here is a re-write of how the answer would look in our format (thus maximizing your score):

Example 5-3 (ANSWER #2 to Dying Declaration)

Dying declaration

A statement made by a now unavailable declarant is admissible if: (1) the declarant believed her death was imminent (but need not actually die), and (2) the statement concerned the cause of what she believed to be her impending death.

Here, Betty is unavailable to testify because she is in a coma. Also, she believed death to be imminent because she said her husband "has killed me. . . ." Furthermore, the statement concerned what she believed to be the cause of her impending death because she said "my husband has just stabbed me." Thus, the dying declaration exception will apply and the statement will be admissible at trial.

Answer #2 is much better at applying specific facts to specific parts of the rule. Another way of putting it: each "sub-conclusion" is supported by a fact. The grader knows that the writer is not merely guessing at each conclusion because the writer in Answer #2 showed all of her work.

Another important point about Answer #2 lies in the quoting of Betty's words. Whenever the Bar Examiners put someone's words in quotes, it's always a good idea for you to do the same. If the fact pattern quotes someone's words, you can guarantee that those words are important to the analysis. Moreover, quoting forces you to match up facts with parts of the rule.

Here's another example, this time from criminal law dealing with the entrapment defense. The rule for entrapment is as follows:

Entrapment is a viable defense only if:

(1) the criminal design originated with law enforcement officers, and

(2) the defendant was not predisposed to commit the crime prior to contact by the officer(s).

Here is the relevant portion of the fact pattern (from the February 2008 Bar Exam, Question #4):

> Bill, a 45-year-old male, lives in Glendale, Arizona. He initiates an online relationship with Darla, who is, unbeknownst to Bill, a 39-year-old undercover Phoenix police officer. Bill and Darla never meet face to face, but in chat sessions Darla represents to Bill that she is 14 years old. During the course of online conversations, Bill informs Darla that he enjoys having sexual relationships with teenagers and asks Darla if she is interested in having sex with him. She answers affirmatively. Bill is eager to meet Darla and have sex with her. Darla, assuring Bill that they will be alone, invites Bill to her home so they can have sex. [Bill is later arrested at Darla's home and charged with multiple crimes.]

You now have the relevant rule and the relevant facts. So I invite you to take about five minutes and write out an answer. Remember the format—apply facts to rules within your analysis. After you are done, turn the page and take a look at the answer.

Example 5-4

Entrapment Defense

Entrapment is a viable defense only if: (1) the criminal design originated with law enforcement officers, and (2) the defendant was not predisposed to commit the crime prior to contact by the officer(s).

Here, the criminal design did not originate with law enforcement officers because Bill was the one who "initiated an online relationship" with Darla. Also, Bill likely *was* predisposed to the crime because he "enjoys having sexual intercourse with teenagers." Thus, entrapment is not a viable defense.

How does your answer compare to the model answer? Hopefully, your answer compares favorably because this is the only answer. And it's a good model to parallel. Notice again the matching of facts to elements of the rule. Plug into the format, and you force yourself into a good model of analysis. Below is a recap of some of the most important points we've covered so far.

A Quick Recap—The Least You Need to Know about Writing Your Analyses

- You do NOT get any credit for merely listing facts.
- My rule of thumb: never list a fact unless you are "analyzing" it—which means integrating facts with rules.
- Don't *list* facts, *integrate* them into the analysis.
- Match up specific facts with specific parts of the rule that govern the issue you are discussing.
- If the fact pattern quotes someone's words, those words are important. Most of the time you will want to quote them back in your analysis.

- You have to state the obvious to get credit for knowing the obvious.
- Show all of your work!

6

Noreuil's Top Ten Tips & Strategies for Essay Writing

In the previous chapters I've outlined specific writing strategies for writing out your analyses. Here are other writing tips and strategies to help maximize your score. I call them my "Top Ten Tips & Strategies" for essay writing.

(1) Before the Exam, Know the "Big Ticket" Topics

By looking at past exams (and/or reading this book) you should have a good idea as to what subjects are tested most often. Know these going into the exam, and devote practice time to these topics. For example, in torts, negligence has been tested eight (8) times in the past ten (10) exams. In evidence, hearsay has been tested on every one of the past ten exams. The issue of an attorney's conflict of interest has been tested on nearly half of the exams.

On a similar note, it is rare that "lesser-tested" topics will be tested on back-to-back exams. I am not, however, in any way, shape or form suggesting that you should ignore topics that were tested on the most recent bar exam. But, at the same time, it's good to be aware of patterns of subjects tested. For example, in evidence, the "best evidence rule" was tested in February 2006, February 2007, July 2007, and July 2008. In contracts, promissory estoppel was tested February 2005, July 2006, July 2007, and July 2008.

In Appendix B I have listed all of the issues that have been tested more than 25% of the time since the February 2003 exam for the Arizona essay questions. Additionally, I have listed the specific exam dates in which those issues were tested. Know the issues most tested (the "big ticket" topics) and look for patterns to see what is likely to be on your exam. Of course, given the changes to the Arizona bar exam in July of 2011, it's also a good idea to check out all of the MEE issues/topics tested.

(2) Pick a Side and Write Your Analysis Accordingly

Unless the facts beg for it, don't worry so much about point, counter-point, counter-counter-point style of writing. Most every issue has a definite conclusion, so write your analysis accordingly. In the course of tutoring, I have too often seen examinees "stretching" to make a counterargument because they thought they were supposed to "give both sides." Don't get too caught up in this.

Of course, if there is a viable counterargument to make, then you should certainly make one. If you do make a counterargument, be sure to resolve the ultimate issue in the end. To put it another way, be sure to resolve the issue of why the counterargument ultimately fails. Do realize, however, that counterarguments are more the exception than the norm on your bar essays.

(3) Be Definitive When Giving Conclusions

Related to our first tip, be conscious of being definitive when giving your ultimate conclusions. Over the course of my years of tutoring, I have seen too many "wishy-washy" conclusions—all of which leave the grader unhappy. Try to avoid using words such as "may" or "possibly" in your final conclusion. Here are a few examples:

> Thus, the evidence may be admissible.
> Thus, it's possible that John might win a negligence claim against Bill.
> Thus, John may have committed the crime of arson.
> Thus, it's arguable that the will is valid.

Again, the bar exam essays almost always have a "correct" conclusion. Be definitive to be most effective. Sometimes, an examinee is reluctant to be definitive because he isn't sure of the conclusion. If this is the case, use your best judgment and pick an outcome. The words "likely" or "unlikely" are effective modifiers. Below are rewrites of the previous "wishy-washy" examples:

> Thus, the evidence is likely admissible.
> Thus, it's unlikely that John will win a negligence claim against Bill.
> Thus, John likely committed the crime of arson.
> Thus, it's likely that the will is valid.

Note that you can get substantial credit for the wrong conclusion—this is where the "analysis" comes into play. In fact, here is a quote from the National Conference of Bar Examiners:

> "Appropriate credit is given in the grading of essay answers for well reasoned analyses of the issues and legal principles involved even though the final conclusion itself may be incorrect."

Again—well reasoned analyses are those that APPLY facts to law. If your analyses flow well, you can still get substantial credit for the wrong conclusion—so be definitive and confident.

(4) Try to Sound Like a Lawyer

You are going through this exam to be admitted to the practice of law—so try to sound like a lawyer whenever possible. Use verbs that lawyers use. For example, don't write that the court should "reject" the petition; write that the court should *dismiss* the petition. Similarly, you don't want to write that the prosecutor's objection should be "denied"; you want to write that it should be *overruled.* But a judge doesn't "overrule" a default judgment, a judge *vacates* a default judgment. A police officer doesn't "take" drugs; an officer *seizes* drugs.

In a similar vein, be sure to use "terms of art" to sound more "lawyer-like." For example, on an evidence question, don't write that a statement was a "contradictory statement to what the defendant said earlier"; write that it was a *prior inconsistent statement.* On a wills question, if you are discussing a child who was born after the execution of the decedent's will, refer to the child by her legal moniker—a *pretermitted* child. You are getting ready to be a lawyer—so be sure to sound like one on the bar exam in order to maximize your score.

(5) Look for Verbal Clues in the Fact Pattern

Look for verbal clues that will give rise to issues—because they are often present in the fact patterns. For example, if the word "precluded" is used in a civil procedure question that might mean collateral estoppel comes into play. If the phrase "relied upon" is used in a contracts question, it might be begging for a promissory estoppel analysis.

Additionally, if the word "admitted" is used to describe what one party to a lawsuit said in evidence, think about party admissions or statements against interest under the rules for hearsay exceptions. If someone "orally agrees" to a contract, you might be looking at a statute of frauds issue. If a statute is involved in a torts question, think about negligence per se. Every word matters—so read critically.

Moreover, pay close attention to ages (especially in a contracts question, because a minor cannot legally enter into a contract with a merchant). Look for words that comprise part of the law—e.g., someone acting "mistakenly" or "unreasonably" or "without authority." Dates can also be important—and not the kind that involve dinner and a movie.

(6) Answer the Specific Question Asked

This is something mentioned earlier that deserves elaboration—because it happens so often on bar exams. Don't waste time trying to impress the graders with all of the esoteric and arcane information you know about a particular subject. You will NOT get credit for gratuitously added information—no matter how esoteric the information is. ANSWER THE SPECIFIC QUESTION ASKED.

I often see examinees giving what I refer to as a "brain dump" on certain essay answers. A "brain dump" is exactly what you think—dumping a bunch of rules that aren't relevant to the question. Resist this temptation. It is better to write nothing and move on to the next subject (as opposed to writing about the evolution of a particular legal rule). Remember—time is at a premium.

(7) Answer Sub-Questions in the Order They Are Presented

Within a particular subject, the call of the question may ask several specific questions. (Evidence questions, in particular, break up the overall "question" into subparts.) If so, answer them in the order they are asked. The graders' "grading rubric" will be in the same order as the enumerated sub-questions, so that's the way you should answer them. Here are a few examples:

The first example is from the July 2004 Bar Exam, Question #10 (Contracts). Here is the call of the question:

1. Is there a valid contract, and if so, what are its terms?
2. If a valid contract exists, is either side in breach? Explain your answer.
3. What, if any, remedies are available to the parties?

In the above example, you would want to answer each question in the same order it is presented. You might feel better (e.g., more knowledgeable) about responding to the "remedies" part of the question, but resist the temptation to answer out of order. Your goal is to make the grader happy.

Here is another example from the July 2006 Bar Exam, Question #8 (Professional Responsibility):

> Please discuss the following issues:
> 1. Did Leon violate any of the Arizona Rules of Professional Conduct in his representation of Alberto and Beatrice during the formation of AZ Software Development Corporation?
> 2. Should Leon have informed Beatrice about his conversation with Alberto?

Again, you may be tempted to answer the second part of the question first—perhaps because you "know it" better. Regardless, answer in the order the question outlines. The above examples may appear obvious as to the order in which you would write out your answer, but other questions may be much more tempting to answer "out of order."

For example, evidence questions very often enumerate three (or four) items of evidence that are being offered at trial (and usually objected to by opposing counsel). If this is the case, you are asked to address the potential for admissibility of each item of evidence.

Answer them in the order they are presented—even if you know #3 the best.

Here is an example from an evidence question—just to make sure you can visualize what I'm talking about. This example is from the July 2006 Bar Exam, Question #5 (Evidence):

> Albert is on trial in Yuma, Arizona for the murder of Ben, his former business associate. Albert was president and Ben was the chief financial officer of Alcorp, Inc.
>
> During its case-in-chief, the prosecution offered evidence that Albert confessed to shooting Ben. During the defense case-in-chief, Albert testified that he shot Ben in self-defense when Ben suddenly and without provocation attacked Albert with a letter opener. The prosecution then presented the following evidence in rebuttal:
>
> 1. A handwritten note found on Albert's desk. The note purports to be from Ben and is addressed to Ben's secretary. The note stated, "I have just discovered that Albert lied to stockholders about the company's finances on the financial statements that I certified as correct. I know I could go to jail, but I intend to call the SEC." Ben's secretary testified that the note could be in Ben's handwriting, but that she is not sure.
> 2. A certified copy of a conviction of Albert for manslaughter, a felony, arising out of a drunk driving incident eight years ago.
> 3. Testimony from Ben's priest, who stated he has known Ben for 20 years and that in his opinion, Ben was a gentle, non-violent person who was "as honest as the day is long."
>
> What objections should Albert raise to the admission of this rebuttal evidence? Discuss how the court should rule on those objections. Assume there is no issue as to whether the evidence is properly offered in rebuttal.

The above example is typical of most every evidence question. Just remember to make it easier on the grader and answer each part of the question in the order it is presented—regardless of which part of the question you may "know" the best.

(8) Short-Cuts

A. Repeating Rules

On the time-pressured bar exam, you oftentimes need a short-cut. If you have occasion to repeat a rule that governs a particular issue, you can just write "See Rule Above." Of course, if you type your answer, you can just copy and paste. Repeating rules often comes into play in evidence, where you may have to give the rule for relevance three times when discussing three different pieces of evidence. Regardless of typing or writing, if you repeat rules, **be sure to give the application of that rule for each issue.** It's not enough just to say "See Rule Above" if you don't have any application.

B. Use a Short-Cut for Rule Explanations

If time becomes an issue (and it often does), you might have to use short-cuts during certain essays. The best place to do this is during your "rule explanations." Oftentimes a rule of law will contain a word or phrase that needs to be defined (also known as a "rule explanation" or a "rule within a rule"). If this happens, and you are running short on time, a parenthetical explanation defining the word or phrase might be your best bet. Of course, in an ideal world, you won't have time constraints and won't need to take any short cuts, but the bar exam doesn't take place in an ideal world.

Below are two examples. Example 6-1 is a standard "rule" and applicable "rule explanation" for first-degree murder. Note how the second example takes a "short-cut" with the explanation of malice aforethought.

Example 6-1 (from criminal law)

> First-degree murder is the unjustified killing of another with malice aforethought and causation. Malice aforethought means acting purposefully or knowingly.

Example 6-2 (from criminal law)

> First-degree murder is the unjustified killing of another with malice aforethought (acting purposefully and knowingly) and causation.

The second example is from contracts. We all know that the "rule" for contract formation requires a valid offer, acceptance, and consideration. Sometimes, however, the "rule explanation" of one or more of those terms is critical to analyzing the problem. Example 6-3 shows a standard rule and rule explanation, while Example 6-4 illustrates the rule explanation short-cut in the parenthetical phrases.

Example 6-3 (from contracts)

> A contract requires offer, acceptance, and consideration. An offer is a promise containing specific and definite terms. Acceptance must be unequivocal and mirror the terms of the offer. Consideration is a bargained for exchange.

Example 6-4 (from contracts)

> A contract requires offer (a promise of specific and definite terms), acceptance (unequivocally mirroring the terms of the offer), and consideration (a bargained for exchange).

Again, I would only suggest using this type of short cut if you are pressed for time. The "short cut" I propose here won't save you twenty minutes, but it might save you enough time at the end to write out one more issue, or one more application—which might just get you the additional point or two you need to pass.

(9) If You Are Struggling with a Particular Area of Law, Try a Hornbook

Hornbooks are great for immersing yourself in a subject and getting a feel for how concepts are interrelated. Of course, you can also ask your peers or old law school professors for recommendations on specific sources. Sometimes, talking through it with someone who has a good grasp on the subject will make things click, too.

With twelve essay topics, it will be difficult to feel you have "mastered" all twelve before the exam. Accept this, and do the best you can on the subjects that give you trouble. Do not, however, make the mistake of devoting an inordinate amount of time to any one subject. It's fine to take a little extra time to try to "get" a particular subject, but don't devote an entire week to it.

(10) After You Answer a Question, LET IT GO

This may be number ten on the list, but I cannot overstate how important it is to be focused during the exam—which means you cannot dwell on any of your previous answers. Once you have answered a question, let it go and move on. Thinking about how poorly (or how well) you did on a previous essay will only detract from your focus.

It's likely that there will be a question or two that throws you for a loop. Know this going into the exam, answer each question the best you can, and move onto the next question with your full attention and focus. Be present at every moment of the bar exam—

don't think about past questions or future questions. Stay in the moment as often as you can, and if you find your mind drifting to the past or the future, let the thought go and bring your attention back to the present.

What the Graders Say

A recent survey of bar essay graders conducted by the NCBE found that the single biggest mistake examinees make is not responding to the specific call of the question. This just reinforces the importance of reading the call of the question first—and last. Remember—don't just "brain dump" all you know about a particular subject or issue; answer the specific call of the question.

7

Studying for the Essay Portion of the Arizona Bar Exam

I've spent the first six chapters outlining how to write your essays. Knowing exactly how to study for the exam is equally important. This chapter deals with how to study for the essay portion of the Arizona Bar Exam. Of course, you must now be prepared for both an "Arizona" essay and an "MEE" essay. It's likely the majority of essays will be MEE essays written by the NCBE, but you also need to prepare for strictly Arizona essays.

First—DO PRACTICE ESSAYS. This should go without saying, right? If you want to be good at anything, it is absolutely critical that you practice. But "how" you practice is often much more important than "how much" you practice. Don't just practice writing essays—practice *correctly*.

At the outset, I wouldn't suggest doing practice essays until you know the law on a given subject. Otherwise, it could just be a waste of time. When you feel well-versed on a particular subject, then you can start writing essays.

To get the most out of your practice essays, be sure to do every essay under test conditions. This means doing practice essays without any distractions—no phone, no TV, no snacking, no pets sitting on your lap. And, as best you can, try to focus on the task at hand as if it were the real thing. The more you can simulate the actual exam, the better off you will be.

Keep track of your time on every practice essay. Only do essays under the same time pressures you will have for the exam. Write down your start time and finish time for every essay. This will give you a gauge for each subject as to how you are doing (and if you need to cut down on your time). It will also give you an idea as to which specific subjects you finish on time and which you have trouble completing within thirty minutes.

At first, it's okay to go over your allotted thirty minutes when doing practice essays. Write until you are done. This will give you a more accurate gauge of your timing. Moreover, it will give you the full amount of practice you need. Perhaps you will find that you are always under thirty minutes on torts, but always over time on civil procedure. Knowing this information may prove invaluable when you actually take the bar exam.

Writing the answer, however, is only the first part of your practice. The other part is reviewing the model answers. If you take a bar review course (or buy the books), every essay will have a model answer. If you just practice with old Arizona released essays, there are "issue summaries" available for your review. The NCBE also writes "model answers" to all of its old essay questions.

Take the time to note each issue, each rule, and each fact application. Figure out where you are deficient. Are you having more problems with issue spotting, or with giving the full rules of applicable law? If you have taken to the idea of the energy notebook I mentioned in Chapter 3, you might want to write down all of the rules you missed for each essay.

As you progress, the best thing to do would be multiple essays back-to-back. Work your way up: two in a row one week, and then three or four in a row the next week. Again, it's key to track your time. The more you can train your brain and simulate test conditions, the better off you will be. In fact, a week or two before the exam, I would recommend doing a full day mock essay exam to see how you hold up under pressure, fatigue, and time constraints. Practice won't make perfect, but with enough, it will make passing.

8

Subject-Specific Tips for the Arizona Essays

Having reviewed every Arizona exam (and "Issue Summary") since 2003 (and several exams even before that), I have come across several points that the graders emphasize, and/or want you to elaborate on. This chapter breaks down each Arizona subject and notes some of these points—many of which may not be obvious at first glance.

Arizona Constitutional Law

- Watch out for issues dealing with standing and Congressional power under the Commerce Clause.

Community Property

- Inception to title doctrine is often tested. [The character of an asset as separate property or community property is determined *at the time the asset is acquired* and the general rule (with a few exceptions) is that subsequent events or expenditures (e.g., payment of remaining purchase price with community funds, using community funds to make improvements, etc.) NEVER affect the asset's characterization, but go only to the possibility of a reimbursement claim and equitable share of enhanced value.]

- For open-ended questions, consider analyzing spousal support—especially if the call of the question asks you to discuss the "distribution of all assets and debts."
- Marital infidelity is ***often*** tested. It's an easy throw-in fact (as the impetus for the divorce). Even though this doesn't factor into the property distribution equation, tell the grader that you know this: "Arizona is a no-fault state, and thus, John's marital infidelity will not affect the property distribution."
- Circle all assets that could possibly be at issue when reading the facts. Community property is usually very straight-forward, but contains several different types of assets and debts, some of which may be easy to overlook.
- Remember that a bank or other financial institution may be an interested party that has a stake in how the assets are distributed.

Criminal Law

- Always consider "attempt" crimes for criminal law questions (e.g., armed robbery and attempted armed robbery).
- Remember: Battery is not a crime in Arizona.
- Remember: Duress is not a defense to a homicide crime.
- Remember: Unlike the common law, someone can be convicted of felony murder in Arizona if a co-felon is killed during the commission of the crime.
- If murder is involved and you are going to address varying degrees of murder (e.g., first-degree, second-degree, manslaughter), always start with first-degree murder and work your way down. This is true even if you think first-degree is not the most likely outcome. The grader's "grade sheet" will be structured similarly.

Criminal Procedure

- If the question involves a Fourth Amendment search and seizure issue, always consider/analyze whether a defendant (or other party) has standing to challenge the searched location and seized item(s). Again, even if it's obvious that the party does have standing, be sure to note this in a quick analysis.

Evidence

- With hearsay, always consider other reasons why something might be offered (e.g., other than for the truth of the matter asserted).
- If anyone makes a statement (as in, words set off by quotation marks), break statements apart to see if one part could be admissible and another part not admissible.
- Always address whether something would be admissible for impeachment purposes if the defendant (in a criminal trial) would take the stand—even if the question fails to mention the defendant might take the stand.
- As a corollary to the above, whenever a party's specific words form part of the analysis, be specific as to what *exactly was said* (rather than just saying "Here, A's statement was made ...").
- Hearsay and relevance are almost always tested. Have a "stock answer" ready that you could recite in your sleep and have a template ready for giving an application thereto. Remember—every piece of evidence must first be relevant to be admissible.
- Present sense impression is often tested.

Contracts

- When appropriate (which is often) begin by giving the governing law: UCC or common law. Memorize your opening blurb—and don't forget to give an actual analysis. For example, don't just write, "The UCC applies to the sale of goods. Goods are moveable objects. Here, the UCC will apply." Instead, be sure to "show all of your work"—even though it's obvious. "The UCC applies to the sale of goods. Goods are moveable objects. Here, the contract is for goods because apples are moveable objects. Thus, the UCC will govern."
- Contract formation is often tested, but do not waste time discussing contract formation if the facts make it clear that the contract is valid.

Civil Procedure

- Watch out for issues of personal jurisdiction, and sanctions.
- There haven't been a lot of "repeat issues" in civil procedure since 2003.

Corporations

- A director's duty of care and duty of loyalty are often tested. If the facts indicate a corporate director is doing something, always think of these two issues.
- Watch out for the *ultra vires* doctrine and piercing the corporate veil—be sure to know the difference and do not confuse the two.
- The business judgment rule is often tested.

Professional Responsibility

- Whenever a question pertains to an attorney violating a rule of professional responsibility, always note the potential discipline she may face.
- Whenever fees are noted, address the reasonability of fees—even if it's obvious that the fees are reasonable.
- If advertising is mentioned in any way, note the rule in Arizona (that allows advertising).
- Duty of competency is an issue that, technically, could always be an "issue" to address. You shouldn't, however, waste time discussing it unless the facts give rise to this duty as a potential issue. For example, if Mary has been a criminal defense attorney her entire life, but then takes on a personal injury case, the issue of duty of competency has been raised and should be addressed.

Property

- Many property questions end with an instruction to "discuss the rights and liabilities of the parties." If this is the case, be sure to organize your answer around the parties (with headings for each specific party).
- Remember to analyze *each act* a party undertakes.
- Know the Recording Act and the effect of a signed but unrecorded deed.

Torts

- Be sure to always, always, always address *comparative fault* analysis under negligence claims (if plausible to fact pattern).

- Whenever a statute is involved in a torts question, think *Negligence per se.*
- Always remember damages in a negligence question—even though it's obvious. Go through each element of a legal theory with the facts to support it (show all of your work!). Example: Here, Paul suffered damages because his arm was broken in the accident.

Wills/Trusts

- As a general rule, if the call of the question asks for an analysis of a will's distribution, always address each party noted in a fact pattern. To make your analysis easier to follow, give each party his/her own separate heading.
- Be specific with dollar amounts whenever possible. Don't just say that "Bill will get half of the specific devise." Note the exact amount Bill will get (whenever possible).
- If a question asks whether a trustee violated his/her fiduciary duty, always consider/analyze each separate act independently.
- Always consider whether capacity might be an issue (but only analyze this if the facts raise it in some way as a potential issue).

9

The Multistate Performance Test ("MPT")

Starting in July 2011, the Arizona Bar Exam became the 27th state to include the Multistate Performance Test (MPT) as part of its bar exam. The MPT will constitute 20 percent of your Arizona bar exam score; the multiple choice (MBE) and essay (MEE) sections will account for 50 and 30 percent, respectively.

The National Conference of Bar Examiners (NCBE) designed the MPT to test "an applicant's ability to use fundamental lawyering skills in a realistic situation." According to the NCBE, the targeted skills are:

- Problem solving
- Legal analysis and reasoning
- Factual analysis
- Communication
- Organization and management of a legal task
- Recognizing and resolving ethical dilemmas[1]

These skills are tested throughout the bar exam, but unlike the MEE and MBE, the MPT does not require you to apply memorized legal rules to a fact pattern. Instead, the materials identify the issue(s) and provide the relevant law. Based on these documents, you are asked to perform a legal task that an attorney should be able to accomplish.[2]

---

1. http://www.ncbex.org/multistate-tests/mpt/mpt-faqs/skills-tested/
2. http://www.ncbex.org/multistate-tests/mpt/mpt-faqs/why/ ("[The MPT] is designed to examine six fundamental skills lawyers are expected to demonstrate regardless of the area of law in which the skills arise.")

Between 1997 and 2010, memoranda were assigned most often (30/69 or 43%), followed by persuasive briefs (19/69 or 28%) and letters (13/69 or 19%).[3] Letters included settlement/demand letters and opinion letters. However, the MPT may contain any lawyering task. The NCBE's illustrative list includes "a statement of facts; a contract provision; a will; a counseling plan; a proposal for settlement or agreement; a discovery plan; a witness examination plan; [and] a closing argument."[4]

In sum, the MPT's goal is to gauge an applicant's ability to "complete a lawyering task within time constraints."[5] Therefore, while it may be less demanding in terms of issue spotting and articulating a rule explanation, the time limits can pose a considerable challenge. You can minimize the impact of time pressure by choosing to approach the MPT with a strategy and a positive attitude.

Arizona will administer the MPT in two 90-minute sessions, with one problem per session. Accordingly, you will have 90 minutes to read 15 to 25 pages of information, organize your response, and competently complete the assigned task. Even if you have never drafted the assigned document, rest assured that your performance on the MPT will not depend on the extent of your experience with a particular format. Rather, familiarity with the test's format is key.

The Materials

The File

The MPT materials will consist of a File and a Library. The first page of the File will contain your instructions, usually in the form of a memorandum from a supervising attorney. This task memo is

3. http://www.ncbex.org/multistate-tests/mpt/
4. http://www.ncbex.org/multistate-tests/mpt/mpt-faqs/description1/
5. http://www.ncbex.org/multistate-tests/mpt/mpt-faqs/description1/

as vital as the call of the question in MEE and MBE fact patterns. It presents the problem and tells you exactly who your client is, what question(s) to address, and which format to use. To further assist you with the layout, the File often includes writing guidelines or an example of the requested written product.

The File contains all of the facts of your case, presented through typical records such as lawyers' notes, memoranda, correspondence, court documents, reports, transcripts, contract provisions, etc. But, along with everything you need to resolve the issue(s), the File includes irrelevant information to more accurately reflect a real-life scenario.

The Library

Generally, the Library includes "cases, statutes, regulations, and rules, some of which may not be relevant to the assigned lawyering task."[6] Consequently, you will need to analyze the issue(s) and identify the applicable law(s). Be aware that the Library represents the only legal authorities available to you in performing the task; you may not rely on extraneous knowledge to answer the question(s). If a Library is not provided, then the File will contain any law needed to resolve the problem.

The Strategy

As I mentioned earlier, adopting a strategy and a positive outlook will enhance your MPT preparation. Your strategy is to practice each MPT problem in an orderly manner that works for you. I have outlined one potential approach below. Training yourself to efficiently move through the checklist will force you to follow a thorough and organized analysis on the day of the exam.

---

6. http://www.ncbex.org/multistate-tests/mpt/mpt-faqs/description1/

1. Read the instructions during practice sessions.
    a. Skim the instructions on exam day.
    b. Read Paragraph 2—Jurisdiction—to identify mandatory versus persuasive authority.
2. Skim the Table of Contents.
    a. What is the main area of law?
    b. Is it a common law or statutory problem?
3. Read the Task Memo.
    a. Identify the problem.
    b. Identify the issues and sub-issues.
    c. What type of document is assigned?
        i. Is it objective or persuasive?
        ii. Are you writing to an attorney or a layperson?
    d. Are any issues expressly excluded from consideration?
4. Read the Instruction Memo, if one is provided.
    a. What structure is required?
    b. If assigned a brief, what components must you include?
        i. Statement of facts?
        ii. Jurisdiction?
        iii. Persuasive subject headings?
    c. Is an example provided?
5. Read the Library.
    a. Cases first, from least to most recent.
        i. Note if any case is overruled.
        ii. Note the level of authority for each.
        iii. Skim the facts for context.
        iv. Extract the rule.
            1. Is it element based?
            2. Is synthesis required?
            3. Is there a multi-prong test?
        v. Check for footnotes! They often contain valuable information.
    b. Review the statutes, codes, and commentaries.
6. Read the File.
    a. Note the relationship of the parties.

   b. Note relevant facts based on the applicable rule(s).
7. Create a Rule Outline:
   a. Mirror the rule structure in a Rule Outline, leaving space for facts.
   b. Write the issue above your Rule Outline.
   c. Add facts to the Rule Outline.
8. Revisit the Task Memo. Does your Outline:
   a. Address each issue?
   b. State relevant facts?
   c. Cite to relevant law(s)?
   d. Apply the law to the facts?
   e. Cite and distinguish contrary authority?
9. Revisit the Instruction Memo to comply with format and technical requirements.
10. Compose!

Of course, all general principles of sound legal writing apply—be direct, be concise, and use plain English. Moreover, always address the specific question(s)/legal issue(s) you are being asked to address. You will not get any additional points for noting extraneous information you remember from law school.

10

The Multistate Bar Exam ("MBE")

This portion of the book will discuss how to prepare and study for the MBE. Specifically, I'll discuss how to study for the MBE. I'll discuss how the questions are constructed, and how to break apart and analyze an MBE question. I will also discuss specific strategies and useful tips for maximizing your MBE score. First, a little background on the MBE.

The Multistate Bar Examination (or "MBE") is an objective six-hour examination containing 200 questions. The examination is divided into two periods of three hours each, one in the morning and one in the afternoon, with 100 questions in each period. In Arizona, the MBE counts for 50% of your overall score.

The examination includes questions in the following areas: Constitutional Law, Contracts, Criminal Law and Procedure, Evidence, Real Property, and Torts. There are 34 questions each in Contracts and Torts and 33 questions each in Constitutional Law, Criminal Law and Procedure, Evidence, and Real Property.

So ... what exactly is tested under each of the seven major subjects? The National Conference of Bar Examiners' website provides you with topic (and sub-topic) coverage for each subject. The website address is: www.ncbex.org. If you click on "MBE" on the left-hand side, it will bring you to the MBE page and you can click on subject matter outlines. These outlines cover everything that could be tested per subject.

Moreover, the outlines give you the percentile breakdown of what's covered per subject. For example, the topic of negligence comprises approximately 50% of the 34 Torts MBE questions. For contracts, approximately 25% of the questions are UCC questions. I encourage you to check it out and get a feel for which topics are tested more commonly than others. Remember—awareness is the key.

One important thing to keep in mind as you study for the MBE: this is a nation-wide test. The multiple choice questions will not be specific to Arizona law. As such, ignore any Arizona distinctions. Also remember that the questions are presented in a random manner, meaning all six subjects are interspersed together throughout the exam.

The NCBE Says …

According to the National Conference of Bar Examiners ("NCBE"), the purpose of the MBE is to assess the extent to which an examinee can apply fundamental legal principles and legal reasoning to analyze a given fact pattern. The questions focus on the understanding of legal principles rather than the memorization of substantive law.

Before we break down and dissect the MBE, I think it's useful to dispel a few myths about the MBE. According the NCBE, the following are all UNTRUE myths about the MBE and the bar exam in general, as noted on the NCBE website:

1. The MBE is a "multiple guess test" for which there are no right answers.
2. If you study only for the MBE and get a high score, you don't need to worry about the rest of the exam.
3. Bar examiners seek to maximize the number of failing examinees.
4. Passing in July is more likely than in February.
5. Answering 100s upon 100s of MBE questions is all you need to do to be prepared for the MBE.

If you have any questions, you can contact the NCBE at the address, phone number or email below. Additionally, the NCBE website contains a great deal of information, including sample MBE questions. The website address is: www.ncbex.org.

National Conference of Bar Examiners
302 S. Bedford Street
Madison, WI 53703-3622
Telephone: (608) 280-8550
Fax: 608-280-8552
TDD: 608-661-1275
E-mail: contact@ncbex.org

How to Study for the MBE

Above all, you have to know the law to do well on the MBE. I talked extensively about learning theory and different strategies for learning the law earlier in the book, so I won't repeat everything here. (For a refresher, see Chapter 3.) Figure out what learning style works best for you, and use it.

Much of the law you will need to know for the MBE will be similar to Arizona law. But it's important to always remember that there are many distinctions between the law tested on the MBE and Arizona law. For example, in Arizona, there is no crime of battery. On the MBE, however, there might be a question dealing with battery. Thus, it's important to know what you are studying—Arizona law for the essay portion, or the law as you need to know it for the MBE.

Knowing the law is the first step to doing well on the MBE, but it is by no means the only step. The questions on the MBE are designed to test your ability to critically analyze a fact pattern vis-à-vis the applicable law. Accordingly, knowing how to study for the MBE is critical to your success.

First—do practice questions. Do as many as you can. You can get questions (and annotated answers) from your bar review course, and from the National Conference of Bar Examiners. The bar examiners will often release old MBE questions. Additionally, you can pay $26 for a sample of 100 MBE questions (with annotated answers) that are actually written by the same people who write the MBE questions. To do this, go to http://www.ncbex.org/mbe-ap.

You want to spend a lot of your study time doing practice questions. But "doing" practice questions cannot be a means to an end. You cannot just "do" 34 questions, check the answers and be done. This is one time when quality really does win out over quantity. It is important to know why the correct answer choice is correct—but it is equally (if not more) important to know why the incorrect answers are wrong.

For every question that you do, read each annotated answer and see not only why the correct answer is correct, but also why the incorrect answers are incorrect. I cannot stress this enough (which is why I repeated it from above). Why is this important? It's important because when you understand why answers are incorrect, you start to see patterns emerging as to how some answers can throw you off.

The MBE, like all multiple choice tests, often comes down to a process of elimination. In fact, sometimes you will pick an answer not because you know that it is correct, but because you know the other three answers are NOT correct. And once you are familiar with why wrong answers are wrong, they are much easier to eliminate.

Starting the MBE Study Process

At first, I recommend practicing one subject at a time. If you divide your MBE sessions into a certain number of questions, do all of the questions from the subject that you have been studying that day. Immersing yourself in a subject can help make connections between interrelated concepts, as well as reinforce learning.

Before you begin any practice session, I would suggest taking time to go over your outline on that particular subject to get in the right frame of mind. If it's torts day, get in the torts frame of mind.

I suggest keeping an MBE log for each subject. Write down the number correct every time you do practice questions for each subject. See what your percentage correct is for each subject, and see what subjects are a strength for you and which are a weakness. Generally speaking, the target percentage you want to hit is somewhere around sixty-five (65%).

Also, take note if there is a particular sub-issue within each subject that you are continuing to miss. If you can identify that the UCC questions are difficult for you, maybe that is a sign to get some additional study aids on that sub-issue. Or maybe you are always missing questions on custodial interrogation in criminal law. Awareness is key—you are likely not going to be great in every subject, but if you can identify your weaknesses, that's the first step to overcoming them.

Of course, as time draws closer to exam day, it will be a good idea to answer questions in a random fashion because that's how they will come at you on the exam. In fact, I would recommend doing a simulated exam at least once. A "simulated" exam would be in the same format as the bar—100 questions in a mock morning session and 100 questions in an afternoon session (with all of the subjects in random order).

Timing

If you break down the timing of the exam, you have to finish 100 questions in three (3) hours—which equates to 1.8 minutes per question. This translates to about 34 questions per hour. Thus, I suggest doing one-hour sessions of a particular subject when you are ready to start answering questions.

If you need to build your way up to it (or don't have the time for an hour session), you can do 17 questions in thirty minutes. But remember—part of the process is conditioning yourself (both mentally and physically) to be able to do two three-hour sessions of 100 questions each. Accordingly, if you can do one-hour sessions of 34 questions, it will give you a better indication as to how you are holding up. Moreover, it will give you a more accurate indication as to how you are doing with timing.

Whenever you do an MBE session, always take note of your time. Write down your start time and your finish time. Are you within the time you need to be? If not, are you improving on your timing the more you practice? Again—awareness is key to your success. And you cannot be aware if you don't take note of your time. To get an accurate gauge of your timing, be very strict about doing practice questions under test conditions (no phone, no TV).

On the day of the exam, it's a good idea to know exactly where you are in regard to your remaining time. If you use the formula noted above (34 questions per hour), you can write out your "time markers" before you read the first question. For example, if you begin the exam at 9:10, you can quickly write out the following:

Time	Question #
9:40	17
10:10	33
10:40	50
11:10	67
11:40	84
12:10	100

Being aware of exactly where you are during the three-hour marathon will help when you are taking the exam. Of course, in an ideal world, your practice sessions will give you a good idea as to whether time will or will not be an issue on the day of the exam.

You don't want to spend an inordinate amount of time on any one question—they are all worth the same amount of points. If you get bogged down on a question, you probably have no better chance of getting the correct answer if you spend two minutes on it or twenty. If a question is that difficult, answer it and move on.

Do note, however, that no matter how much you practice, it will be difficult to simulate the conditions and emotions you are feeling while taking the actual exam. As such, just because you have always been "on time" during your practice sessions, that doesn't necessarily mean your time will be the same on exam day. Be safe and track your time.

Reviewing Your Practice MBE Questions

After each session, as you "grade" (or "review") all of the annotated answers, try to figure out WHY you missed a particular question. Consider—

1. Did you miss it because you didn't know the applicable law?
2. Did you overlook an important fact?
3. Did you confuse the parties?
4. Did you misapply the facts to the rule?
5. Did you mischaracterize a fact or assume a fact not specifically noted?
6. Did you have a problem focusing?

If the problem was your focus, was it because it was late in the day or was it because you have a mental block with that particular subject (which could be due to an evil law school professor or poor grade, etc.)? If you do have a particular hang-up or negative feeling about a particular subject, try to cozy up to it. Grab a hornbook or try to talk it through with a friend.

Regardless of the reason you missed a particular question, the more you realize *why* you are getting questions wrong, the better chance you have to fix it. And that's what's great about annotated answers—they do help you see where you go awry.

Practice, practice, practice—that is the key to doing well. And not just practicing, but practicing correctly. Treat each session as if you were taking the actual exam. Don't flip to the answers after each question. Simulate test conditions to the best of your ability.

When you grade or review the answers, see why answers are right, see why answers are wrong, look for patterns, figure out why you are missing the ones that you do, gauge your time. And remember—even if you get a question right, you should still check to see why all of the other answers are wrong.

As a final comment on preparation, if at all possible, try to study at the same times every day—preferably the same times you will be taking the exam. It's a marathon, not a sprint, and you are conditioning your brain, so condition it to be focused at the same times that you will be taking the actual exam whenever possible.

Breaking Down the MBE

First and foremost—the MBE is really a reading comprehension test. You have to understand and digest the fact pattern. Second, you have to know the substantive law. But that's just the start.

The real key to the MBE is being able to apply the substantive law to the fact pattern in order to pick the most correct answer. This "art" is often referred to as logical reasoning, and is usually the most difficult part of the MBE. There is one "most correct" answer, and there are usually other, "plausible, but not correct" answers. Again, this is not a test geared toward rote memorization of the law. The application of law to facts is critical.

How MBE Questions Are Constructed

I think it's helpful to understand what the Bar Examiners are thinking when drafting MBE questions. I have reprinted below the Bar Examiners' guidelines for drafting questions as noted on their website (www.ncbex.org).

The Guidelines for Drafting MBE Questions

- The drafters want to focus items on key concepts and principles that are essential for all examinees to understand, and avoid esoteric topics that are not essential.
- The drafters emphasize scenarios that are relevant to practice.
- Their task is to develop well-written scenarios that include clear fact patterns.
- Finally, their goal is to ensure that the question is asking something important, and that any option requires the examinee to make important distinctions.

As you all probably know, you will be given a fact pattern, then asked a specific question, then asked to choose the most correct answer out of four. What you are asked—or the "Call of the Question"—can take various forms, largely depending on the particular subject being tested. Here are a few examples:

a. What is the Plaintiff's most likely theory of recovery?
b. What is the Defendant's best defense to the charges?
c. Does A have a cause of action against B?
d. How should the judge rule on the prosecutor's objection?
e. Which of the following is the most likely outcome in A's suit against B?

Practice will give you intimate familiarity with the various calls of the question, but you probably get the picture from the above examples. Now that you have the context for this portion of the exam, let's dive into some strategies for doing well on the MBE in the next chapter.

11

Strategies for Doing Well on the MBE

Read the Call of the Question First

As with essays, you should read the call of the question first. The call will usually only be a sentence or two, and reading it first won't markedly add to your overall time. There are several reasons to read the call of the question before you read the fact pattern.

First, knowing exactly what is being asked is crucial. Similar to essay writing, reading the call of the question first will help ground you in the subject matter, so you can get in a "contracts" frame of mind when you are reading the question. When you practice, most of the time you will practice a particular subject (such as "torts"). As such, you are already in a "torts frame of mind" for each question of that practice session.

Remember, however, similar to essay questions, the MBE questions come at you randomly and sometimes you won't be sure whether you are reading a contracts, property, or torts question until you get to the call of the question. If, however, you read the call of the question first, you will know what subject is being tested and can approach the facts with that topic in mind (similar to how you practiced).

Reading the call of the question first gives you context as you begin reading the fact pattern. Different facts may take on a different significance for different subjects, depending on exactly what is being asked. As such, the call of the question may help you know exactly what you are looking for in the fact pattern, thereby saving you time.

To illustrate the latter point, sometimes a question will specifically ask you to adopt a particular side's viewpoint—in which case you will want to read the facts with a certain party's interests in mind. Usually (but not always), these types of questions will ask for a side's "best argument." Here are a few examples of what I'm talking about from actual released questions. (I have only listed the calls of the questions and not the entire fact patterns.)

> His best argument for being found NOT guilty is that he ...
>
> The strongest constitutional argument to support Owner's claim is ...
>
> If Fizzy Cola Company sued Happy-Time for breach of their distribution contract, which of the following facts, if established, would most strengthen Fizzy's case?
>
> The strongest ground upon which Concessionaire could challenge the occupancy tax is that it violates the ...
>
> If Baker wins, it will be because ...

As you can see, there are many types of these "best argument" questions. Obviously, it's helpful to know what party you are going to make an argument for before you read the facts, so reading the call of the question is particularly invaluable for these types of questions. Moreover, you can also see that the "call" is often just a single sentence (or less), which shouldn't eat up too much of your time.

Critical Reading—The Fact Pattern

After you have read the call of the question, read the fact pattern, and then read the call of the question again. I realize that time may be a factor, but you have 1.8 minutes per question, and reading the call of the question twice should not markedly add to your time. (In an ideal world, the more you could read the entire question, the better.) You will have a better idea of how many times you can read each fact pattern if you are diligent in tracking your time during practice sessions.

In fact, a common mistake test takers make is to get in such a hurry that they actually misread what is being asked in the call of the question. If you are going to be sure of anything, be sure of *exactly* what is being asked. READING CAREFULLY is key, and reading the call of the question is the biggest part of this key. Furthermore, it should be noted that, for those who have adequately practiced, answering all 100 questions in the allotted amount of time is usually not a problem.

After you have read the call of the question and then read the fact pattern, the next thing you should do is look for the issue. Yes—contrary to what you may believe—issue spotting plays a significant role on the MBE.

Once you know the issue, think about the rule that governs that issue. By knowing exactly what the issue is, and the rule that governs it, you can often eliminate a response or two. This is because often an incorrect answer will give a correct legal rule ... to an inapplicable legal theory (e.g., one that does not govern the issue at hand).

For example, if the "issue" is one of negligence, and one of the answers talks about the rule for *res ipsa loquitor*, that answer choice can be eliminated. If, for example, the "issue" was one of strict liability, and one of the answer choices talked about the "rule" for negligence, then that answer will be incorrect. Remember—just because an answer choice correctly states a legal rule, that doesn't mean it's the best answer for that particular question.

Let's take a look at what I mean by looking at a few questions. The following examples are from past MBE questions that have been released by the NCBE.

MBE SAMPLE QUESTION #1[7]

> Chemco manufactured a liquid chemical product known as XRX. Some XRX leaked from a storage tank on

---

7. The sample MBE questions contained in this book are actual released questions and are copyrighted by the National Conference of Bar

Chemco's property, seeped into the groundwater, flowed to Farmer's adjacent property, and polluted Farmer's well. Several of Farmer's cows drank the polluted well water and died.

If Farmer brings an action against Chemco to recover the value of the cows that died, Farmer will

A. prevail, because a manufacturer is strictly liable for harm caused by its products.
B. prevail, because the XRX escaped from Chemco's premises.
C. not prevail, unless farmer can establish that the storage tank was defective.
D. not prevail, unless Chemco failed to exercise reasonable care in storing the XRX.

Using our "Issue-spot first" method, we identify the issue first. Here, the issue is strict liability (specifically, a possessor of land's strict liability). Then we think about the rule for strict liability and we can easily eliminate answer choices C and D because they both deal with the rule for negligence. Answer C implicitly does so and D overtly does so by giving part of the "rule" regarding negligence—by noting the "failure to exercise reasonable care."

So if you identify the issue first, you can often eliminate an answer or two that deals with a different legal theory—or different "issue." Remember—ISSUES always come from the FACTS. (And, in case you are wondering, B is the correct answer to MBE Sample Question #1.)

Moreover, if an answer choice states part of a rule from a different legal theory (e.g., a theory not at issue from the facts), then you can eliminate it. For example, if a fact pattern gives rise to a Com-

---

Examiners (NCBE) and reprinted herein with permission. No part of any question may be reproduced or transmitted in any form or by any means (including photocopying) unless expressly permitted in writing by the NCBE. The author greatly thanks the NCBE for permission to use the sample questions.

merce Clause issue, and an answer choice gives a rule that pertains to a different constitutional power, you know you can eliminate it. The key is to spot the issue and know the rule of law that governs that particular issue (or legal theory).

Let's look at another example, this one from criminal law:

MBE SAMPLE QUESTION #2

> Despondent over losing his job, Wilmont drank all night at a bar. While driving home, he noticed a car following him and, in his intoxicated state, concluded he was being followed by robbers. In fact, a police car was following him on suspicion of drunk driving. In his effort to get away, Wilmont sped through a stop sign and struck and killed a pedestrian. He was arrested by the police.
>
> Wilmont is prosecuted for manslaughter. He should be
>
> A. acquitted, because he honestly believed he faced an imminent threat of death or severe bodily injury.
> B. acquitted, because his intoxication prevented him from appreciating the risk he created.
> C. convicted, because he acted recklessly and in fact was in no danger.
> D. convicted, because he acted recklessly and his apprehension of danger was not reasonable.

In the question above, the overall issue is clearly stated in the call of the question: manslaughter. Answer A appears to give correct reasoning (Wilmont likely did have an honest belief that he faced an imminent threat of death or severe bodily injury because he thought he was being chased by robbers). The reasoning, however, pertains to the issue of self-defense, not manslaughter. Accordingly, Answer A can immediately be eliminated. (In case you are wondering, the correct answer is "D.")

How do you become an adept MBE issue spotter? The same way you do with essay issue spotting: practice. Just be sure when you practice you are focusing on the FACTS in order to decipher the specific issue.

Eliminating Answer Choices

No matter how much you study for the MBE, you will not know the answer to every question. Moreover, you will be forced to make an educated guess on some of the questions. Being able to eliminate answer choices is critical to doing well on the MBE. Here are a few of the big reasons why answer choices can be wrong (and therefore eliminated):

(1) The answer mischaracterizes the facts—pay attention to detail and, again, critical reading is key.
(2) The answer choice assumes a fact in dispute.
(3) The answer's reasoning is legally incorrect.
(4) The law is stated incorrectly.
(5) The answer applies the minority rule (rather than the majority rule).

As to (5), it is important to know that if a question is silent as to which law to apply (the majority or minority rule), always apply the majority rule. Do note, however, that the MBE does in fact question you on minority rules. Just don't apply them unless you are told to do so in the question.

(6) A rule of law is perfectly stated, but it is inapplicable to the issue raised by the facts.

I alluded to (6) when talking about issues and inapplicable rules of law, but I'd like to re-emphasize this point because it's an important one. Keep an eye out for a perfectly stated rule of law that doesn't apply to the given fact pattern. This type of "wrong" answer can really trip you up because you see a perfectly articulated and CORRECT rule of law, and you are looking for the CORRECT answer, so this must be the choice. But, hopefully, now that you are aware of it, you will look to identify an issue (when applicable) and not fall into this trap.

(7) An answer choice can be wrong even if it's a "correct" answer.

The answer choice noted by (7) is a tough one. But it's true—an answer choice can still be "wrong" even if it's factually and legally correct. How could an answer be wrong if it's both legally and factually correct? Remember—we're not looking for a "right" answer, we're looking for the "best" answer. Accordingly, multiple answers could be "correct," but the "most correct" answer is usually more precise and/or contains more reasoning.

Always remember: you are looking for the MOST CORRECT or the BEST answer for that particular fact pattern. This means that **every part** of the answer must be correct for it to be a viable choice:

> It must state the correct law;
>
> It must correctly characterize the facts;
>
> It must have sound application of law to fact—or to put it another way, it must have correct, logical legal reasoning;
>
> And, finally, it (almost always) needs to address and resolve a central issue raised by the fact pattern.

Most of the time the correct answer is not going to jump out at you. The process of elimination is a crucial part of taking (and doing well on) the MBE. Knowing the primary reasons why answer choices can be eliminated will go far toward helping you pass the bar exam. Learn them, live them, love them.

12

Noreuil's Top Ten Tips for the MBE

(1) Don't Ever Assume Facts

Don't ever assume facts or read facts into the fact pattern if they aren't explicitly stated. Unlike law school exams, there are no "omitted facts" in the fact pattern. As such, you should never read into the question facts that aren't there. Similarly, never assume any facts. A fact is either in the fact pattern or it is not. Period.

(2) Assume That Every Fact Is Important

As a corollary to #1, always assume that every fact in every question is important ... because usually it is. Even facts that initially appear to be meaningless are likely to be important. Remember—there are very few red herrings. Accordingly, for the most part (not always, but for the most part), all given facts are important. So treat them as such when reading the fact patterns.

As you read the fact pattern, ask yourself: why might this fact be important? Of course, if you have read the call of the question first (which you will have done because you have read this book), you will have a much better context for figuring out why a particular fact might be important. And, as with the essay portion of the exam, pay particular attention to dates, ages, and dollar amounts. Also be sure to take note of words that describe how a party is acting: knowingly, unknowingly, unconsciously, reasonably, unreasonably, etc.

(3) Avoid Skipping around from Question to Question

Answer the questions in the order they are presented. Skipping questions could result in your answers being mis-marked on the answer sheet—and that is the worst possible thing that can happen on the MBE. Moreover, you likely won't have enough time to pick and choose your preferred subject questions first.

Answer each question in order, and if you have to guess before moving on, then guess, but perhaps put a star by that question so you can come back to it if you have time left over. Furthermore, be sure to answer every question because you are not penalized for wrong answers.

(4) If Two Answers Are Opposite, One Is Probably True

This appears self-evident (and it is), but it brings up a larger point about "opposite answers" that I want to note. Most of the time answer choices will be split among outcomes, with two answers concluding one way and two answers concluding the opposite way. For example, two answer choices will conclude that A is guilty of the charged crime, and two answers that A is not guilty.

There are, however, times when the answer choices are split three-to-one, meaning three answers have one outcome and one answer concludes the opposite way. You may be duped into thinking that whenever this happens, the "correct" answer most likely comes from the group of three answers. Do not make this mistake. In fact, the opposite is often true—the stand alone conclusion is just as likely (if not more likely) to be correct than any of the other three. Here are a few examples of what I mean from past MBE questions:

MBE SAMPLE QUESTION #3

Penstock owned a large tract of land on the shore of a lake. Drury lived on a stream that ran along one boundary of Penstock's land and into the lake. At some time in the past, a channel had been cut across Penstock's land from the stream to the lake at a point some distance from the mouth of the stream. From where Drury lived, the channel served as a convenient shortcut to the lake. Erroneously believing that the channel was a public waterway, Drury made frequent trips through the channel in his motorboat. His use of the channel caused no harm to the land through which it passed.

If Penstock asserts a claim for damages against Drury based on trespass, which of the following would be a correct disposition of the case?

A. Judgment for Penstock for nominal damages, because Drury intentionally used the channel.
B. Judgment for Drury, if he did not use the channel after learning of Penstock's ownership claim.
C. Judgment for Drury, because he caused no harm to Penstock's land.
D. Judgment for Drury, because when he used the channel he believed it was a public waterway.

MBE SAMPLE QUESTION #4

Pawn sued Dalton for injuries received when she fell down a stairway in Dalton's apartment building. Pawn, a guest in the building, alleged that she caught the heel of her shoe in a tear in the stair carpet. Pawn calls Witt, a tenant, to testify that Young, another tenant, had said to him a week before Pawn's fall: "When I paid my rent this morning, I told the manager he had better fix that torn carpet."

Young's statement, reported by Witt, is

A. admissible, to prove that the carpet was defective.

B. admissible, to prove that Dalton had notice of the defect.
C. admissible, to prove both that the carpet was defective and that Dalton had notice of the defect.
D. inadmissible, because it is hearsay not within any exception.

The above are examples of what I call a "three-to-one split." In both cases, the "stand alone" conclusion is correct. (In Question 3, "A" is the correct answer; and "D" is the correct answer in Question 4.) I am, of course, in no way telling you to automatically choose the stand alone answer choice on the MBE. All I am saying is that you should in no way be predisposed to assume that the correct answer will come from the side with the three similar outcomes.

(5) A More Precise Answer Is Usually Better Than a Less Precise Answer

A more "precise" answer is a "better" (and therefore more "correct") answer. A more precise answer either (a) incorporates more facts, (b) covers more issues raised from the question, or (c) gives more reasoning. Here are a few very basic examples:

Example 12-1 (from criminal law)

A. The defendant is not guilty of any crime.
B. The defendant is guilty of a crime because he killed the victim.
C. The defendant is guilty of manslaughter.
D. The defendant is guilty of manslaughter because he killed the victim in the heat of passion.

Example 12-2 (from evidence)

A. The evidence is inadmissible.
B. The evidence is admissible.

C. The evidence is admissible even though it is hearsay.
D. The evidence is admissible under the excited utterance exception to the hearsay rule.

In both examples the last answer is more precise, and thus, technically "more correct" than the other three. (Of course, D may or may not be more correct vis-à-vis Answer A, which has a different result.) Accordingly, D is a better choice than B or C. Here is an example of what I mean from an actual MBE released question:

MBE SAMPLE QUESTION #5

Loomis, the owner and operator of a small business, encourages "wellness" on the part of his employees and supports various physical-fitness programs to that end. Learning that one of his employees, Graceful, was a dedicated jogger, Loomis promised to pay her a special award of $100 if she could and would run one mile in less than six minutes on the following Saturday. Graceful thanked him, and did in fact run a mile in less than six minutes on the day specified. Shortly thereafter, however, Loomis discovered that for more than a year Graceful had been running at least one mile in less than six minutes every day as a part of her personal fitness program. He refused to pay the $100.

In an action by Graceful against Loomis for breach of contract, which of the following best summarizes the probable decision of the court?

A. Loomis wins, because it is a compelling inference that Loomis' promise did not induce Graceful to run the specified mile.
B. Loomis wins, because Graceful's running of the specified mile was beneficial, not detrimental, to her in any event.
C. Graceful wins, because running a mile in less than six minutes is a significantly demanding enterprise.

D. Graceful wins, because she ran the specified mile as requested, and her motives for doing so are irrelevant.

The correct answer is Answer D. Notice how Answer D is more precise—it gives two reasons for why Graceful wins. The other answers only give one reason as to why the court should rule a certain way.

In no way should you base your initial strategy on selecting the more precise answer, but if you come to a sticking point in your analysis, you are more likely to be correct by picking the more precise answer.

(6) Be Very Leery of Absolutes

As you probably know after three years of law school, there are very few absolutes in the law. Thus, there are few absolutes on the MBE. As such, beware of answers that state absolutes with words such as "always" or "never."

(7) Focus on Conjunctions

There are four types of conjunctions that you might encounter on the MBE. It's important to know exactly what each one means when breaking down each answer choice. The four types of conjunctions important in this context are: because, if, only if, and unless. Let me break down what each means as it pertains to the MBE answer choices.

Because

The conjunction "because" is the most common type of connector on the MBE. Here's an example of an answer choice with "because" as its conjunction:

> John will likely prevail because he was unaware of the agreement.

As you can see, the word "because" connects the conclusion with a specific reason for that conclusion. Accordingly, for an answer choice to be the correct answer, both the conclusion ("John will prevail") must be correct, and the reason supporting the conclusion ("because he was unaware of the agreement") must be correct.

If

There's one big thing to remember about the "if" conjunction: the fact that is contained in the "if" answer choice does *not* have to appear in the actual fact pattern. The "if" connector hypothesizes about a new fact not contained in the original fact pattern. Here's an example of an answer choice containing "if":

> John will prevail if he was unaware of the agreement.

For an answer choice to be correct when it contains the conjunction "if" requires that the focus of inquiry be narrowed to whether or not the entire statement is true, with the assumption that the proposition which follows the "if" is true. BUT there is no requirement that facts in the fact pattern support the proposition following the "if" connector.

Only If

The "only if" conjunction is basically the same as the "if" conjunction, but when "only if" is used, the answer choice cannot be correct except when the condition following the word "if" is true. Here's an example:

> John will prevail only if he was unaware of the agreement.

Thus, in the above example, the "only if" connector denotes that the only possible way John can prevail is by showing he was unaware of the agreement. If John can prevail in some other manner in addition to being unaware of the agreement, the above answer choice would be incorrect.

Unless

The conjunction "unless" performs the same logical function as the conjunction "only if" except that it follows a negative result instead of a positive one.

> John will not prevail unless he was unaware of the agreement.

The above example is the same as the example containing the "only if" connector, but it is stated in the negative (by adding the "not" in front of "prevail"). Regardless, the meaning is the same: John can only prevail if he was unaware of the agreement—and there is no other means by which he could prevail.

(8) When All Else Fails—Choose the Longest Answer

I don't recommend this very often, but if you are at a complete loss as to the correct answer, consider choosing the longer answer. All other things being equal, a longer answer probably contains more reasoning—thereby likely making it more "correct." (Note that this tip is closely related to Tip #5: an answer that is more precise or contains more reasoning is usually "longer" than other answers.) And if you couldn't eliminate answers by other means, and it's a choice between two (or even three) answers, pick the longer one. Again—when I say "longer" I mean "more reasoning." Here are a few examples, both of which are actual released questions:

MBE SAMPLE QUESTION #6

> The United States Department of Energy regularly transports nuclear materials through Centerville on the way to a nuclear weapons processing plant it operates in a nearby state. The City of Centerville recently adopted an ordinance prohibiting the transportation of any nu-

clear materials in or through the city. The ordinance declares that its purpose is to protect the health and safety of the residents of that city.

May the Department of Energy continue to transport these nuclear materials through the City of Centerville?

A. No, because the ordinance is rationally related to the public health and safety of Centerville residents.
B. No, because the Tenth Amendment reserves to the states certain unenumerated sovereign powers.
C. Yes, because the Department of Energy is a federal agency engaged in a lawful federal function and, therefore, its activities may not be regulated by a local government without the consent of Congress.
D. Yes, because the ordinance enacted by Centerville is invalid because it denies persons transporting such materials the equal protection of the laws.

In the above example, C is the correct answer. It happens to be the "longest" answer, but it (more importantly) has more reasoning than the other choices (which makes it "longer").

If we enumerate the "reasons" behind each answer, we see that only Answer C actually contains two reasons after the causal connector "because": (1) the Department of Energy is a federal agency engaged in a lawful federal function, and (2) its activities may not be regulated by a local government without the consent of Congress. The other answer choices only offer one reason in support of their conclusion.

Here is another example from a released question:

MBE SAMPLE QUESTION #7

Which of the following fact patterns most clearly suggests an implied-in-fact contract?

A. A county tax assessor mistakenly bills Algernon for taxes on Bathsheba's property, which Algernon, in good faith, pays.

B. Meddick, a physician, treated Ryder without Ryder's knowledge or consent, while Ryder was unconscious as the result of a fall from his horse.
C. Asphalt, thinking that he was paving Customer's driveway, for which Asphalt had an express contract, mistakenly paved Nabor's driveway while Nabor looked on without saying anything or raising any objection.
D. At her mother's request, Iris, an accountant, filled out and filed her mother's "E-Z" income-tax form (a simple, short form).

In the above example, C is the correct answer. Again, it is the "longest" answer—and the one containing the most relevant information to the issue of an implied-in-fact contract. I would like to reiterate that this "tip" should only be used when you are stuck and have exhausted all other avenues of deciding the answer. Choosing the "longest" answer should only be used as a last resort.

No matter how prepared you are, no matter how many practice questions you do, no matter how well you know the law, you will have to guess during the MBE. The key is to make intelligent, educated guesses. And you do that by going through all of the processes that we have talked about and eliminating as many answer choices as you can.

(9) Ask the Universe

If you STILL don't have a clue, then clear your mind completely and ask the universe what the correct answer is ... and whatever pops into your head is what you go with. Hey, the universe always knows—you just have to make sure you are listening. ☺

(10) After Each Question, Let It Go

As noted on the section on essay writing, it is absolutely critical to "let go" of an answer after you have moved on to the next one. Again, lingering thoughts about a particular question will only take your focus away from the next question. And FOCUS and CONCENTRATION throughout the exam are the quintessential keys to getting a passing score.

What the NCBE Says

I have given you my top ten tips, but now I'd like to give you NCBE's "Top Three," as outlined at the October 2007 NCBE Conference in Madison, Wisconsin. According to the NCBE, studies have shown that the top three reasons for incorrect answers on MBE multiple choice questions are:

(1) Errors in knowing or understanding legal principles (you have to know the law).
(2) Errors in assuming facts or reading non-existing facts into the fact pattern.
(3) Not responding to the specific call of the question.

The Least You Need to Know— The Strategy for MBE Questions

- Read the call of the question first;
- Read the fact pattern (and read the call of the question again at the end);
- Even before you look at the answer choices—try to decide the issue;

- Once you know the issue, think about the rule that governs that issue (and, of course, any exceptions to that rule);
- Then, read the answer choices and try to eliminate as many choices as you can;
- If you are clueless between two answers (or more), go with the answer that is more precise, or has more reasoning (which will likely make it a longer answer); and
- Let it go and move on.

13

What You Need to Know Beyond the Law

Before the Exam— Know Your Location

Heretofore, the Arizona Bar Exam has always been administered in either Phoenix or Tucson (usually on a rotating basis). If you have to travel, be sure to get your hotel (or other accommodations) *early*. Be sure to do a "dry run" from your hotel (or residence) to the exam location to see how long it takes to get there. Be sure to do this at the same time you will be traveling to get a feel for traffic at that particular time.

If at all possible, check out the room of the exam location beforehand. It will help you to visualize yourself doing well prior to exam day. It will also give you a "feel" for the place—both energetically and temperature wise. Although they will tell you on the day of the exam, it would also be helpful to know exactly where the bathrooms are located.

Before the Exam— Know the Rules of Protocol

If you don't know the rules, it could cost you. One of the rules of the Arizona Bar Exam is that you cannot take your exam past certain points in the examination room (and for good reason, such as to discourage cheating). A former student told me a story about an examinee who (apparently inadvertently) got up and took part of his exam past the restricted area and was immediately excused from the exam.

Another rule to keep in mind—do not bring your cell phone! You will get a complete list of all of the rules after you have sent in your application and fee to sit for the bar exam. Read the rules a few times before the exam, know the rules, and abide by them.

The Day of the Exam

It's game time, so put on your game face. Hopefully, you took my advice and cut down on the caffeine during the lead-up to the exam. It's an awful idea to load up on caffeine the morning of the exam. For one, you will experience the caffeine "crash" right around the middle of the first exam session. Also, you don't want to waste time taking multiple bathroom breaks during the exam.

Eat well, but not too much. The earlier you eat, the better. You want to give your food time to digest before sitting down for three hours of thinking and writing.

Wear comfortable clothes. I know it's hot in Arizona, but it may be exceedingly cool in the examination location. As such, shorts aren't really a good idea (nor are flip flops). You don't want to be distracted because you are cold (or hot). That is why long pants (sweats, khakis, comfortable jeans) and layers on top work well.

Bring your outlines with you on Day 1—the essay day—so that you can go over them during the two-hour lunch break. You will want to use this time to switch mental gears from the MPT to essay writing, and looking over your outlines is a good way to do this. Speaking of lunch, be sure to again eat well—eat something healthy, not too filling. Avoid foods that make you sleepy (turkey, milk, etc.). Moreover, avoid talking about the first session with your friends. Doing so will only feed your anxiety.

After Day 1, take some time to decompress. You will be doing yourself a disservice if you immediately start studying for the next day's MBE exam. Try to relax, clear your mind, have a good (healthy) dinner. And, above all else, don't look back. In fact, make it a point to avoid anyone who wants to talk to you about specific questions or "issues" from the essay portion. Get a good night's sleep and stay positive.

Concluding Remarks

I hope you have found the information in the book helpful. Regardless of how well you absorb and implement the strategies and tactics of this book, there are certain things you have to do if you want to pass. I know it's a daunting task, but do your best to be optimistic and appreciate the opportunity that you "get to" study for the bar exam. Optimists are more successful,[8] so choose to be optimistic about the process, choose to be optimistic about passing. Study hard (it's now your job!), practice correctly, eat well, exercise, sleep well, be focused, be positive, be confident ... and pass the bar exam. Good luck—and happy passing. ☺

8. *See generally*, Martin Seligman, *Learned Optimism: How to Change Your Mind and Your Life*, Pocket Books (1998).

Appendices

Appendix A— A Note to Repeat Takers

It is my sincere hope that you do not have to read this section. If you did not pass the exam, you can pass the next time—or even the time after that. (I tutored one person who had failed four times before he came to me, and then passed the fifth time with points to spare.)

There are two critical things to do in order to pass as a repeat taker. First, let go of the stigma or embarrassment you might feel because you didn't pass the exam. You are not alone—thousands of people across the country are unsuccessful the first, second or even third time they take the exam. Sometimes, as many as 40% of the Arizona examinees do not pass.

Not passing should in no way be equated with your level of intelligence. Most people fail the exam because they don't know how to take the time-pressured test. If you made it into law school and graduated, you are smart enough to pass the exam. Let go of any hit to your confidence or ego, and learn how to study correctly, and how to actually take the exam. I hope this book has helped in both of these endeavors.

If you want to pass this time, the second most important thing to do is this: do something different. Obviously, whatever you did as far as preparation and taking the exam didn't work last time, so do something different. Study more, study more efficiently, do more MBEs, more practice essays, etc. Try a different bar prep course, read books on how to take the exam, and/or hire a tutor.

Whatever you do differently, it is absolutely critical that you pinpoint your weaknesses on your old exam. Find out as much as you can about what went wrong. Ask yourself: How did my MBE score compare with my essay score?

Is there a high correlation between the two, or was I completely deficient in one area and not the other? How much did exam day anxiety factor into my performance?

Regardless of your essay scores (even if they were high), you want to improve in every area you can. To that end, as quickly as possible, contact the Arizona Bar Examiners and order copies of your old essays. You will get a copy of the questions, your answers, and the "issue summaries." From there, it should be relatively obvious where you went wrong—was it issue spotting, knowing the law, or applying the law? Most of the time, it's some combination thereof, but you should be able to isolate the biggest problem.

Ask yourself this question: did I truly know the law? If the answer is yes, then perhaps writing and analysis is the area you need to improve the most. Whenever possible, try to look for "model" answers. Arizona does not release model answers, but you can often find "model" answers from bar review courses.

Remember, many people fail the bar exam and pass the second (or third, or fourth) time around. And you can, too. If you want it badly enough, and if you believe it strongly enough, you will pass. Good luck and happy passing.

Appendix B— Recent Topics Tested on the Arizona Essay Exam

The following is a list of topics/issues tested (by subject) on the Arizona essay exam from July 2003–July 2010 and the exam dates in which they were tested. (Only topics tested at least 25% of the time are noted.)

AZ Civil Procedure

Notice pleading (ARCP 8(a)(2) requirements & purpose): 27%—Feb. '04, July '06, July '07, July '09.

Federal Civil Procedure (MEE—percentages omitted)

Personal jurisdiction: July '09, July '10.

Notice pleading (FRCP 8(a)(2) requirements): July '09, July '10.

AZ Constitutional Law

Congress's powers under the Commerce Clause: 27%—July '03, July '04, Feb. '05, Feb. '10.

Community Property

Distinguishing between separate and community property: 80%—July '03, Feb. '04, July '04, July '05, Feb. '06, July '06, July '07, Feb. '08, July '08, Feb. '09, July '09, Feb. '10.

Distinguishing between separate and community property/inheritance: 33%—July '03, Feb. '04, July '07, July '08, July '09.

Distinguishing between separate and community property/account in one party's name: 27%—July '03, Feb. '04, July '04, July '08.

Distinguishing between separate and community debt/educational loan incurred by one party prior to marriage: 27% —July '03, July '04, July '05, Feb. '09.

Distinguishing between separate and community property/property (paychecks) acquired after service of petition for dissolution of marriage: 27%—July '03, Feb. '05, July '09, Feb. '10.

General rules for division of property upon divorce: 67%—July '03, Feb. '04, July '04, July '06, Feb. '07, July '07, Feb. '08, Feb. '09, July '09, Feb. '10.

Court's consideration of an extramarital affair: 60%—July '03, July '04, Feb. '05, July '05, July '06, Feb. '07, July '07, July '08, July '09.

Validity of a marriage: 33%—Feb. '05, July '05, July '07, July '08, Feb. '10.

Enforcement of a pre-marital agreement: 33%—July '03, July '04, Feb. '06, Feb. '08, Feb. '10.

Binding the community to an obligation by one spouse (real estate property/lease): 27%—Feb. '04, Feb. '08, July '09, Feb. '10.

Contracts

When Arizona UCC applies: 47%—July '03, Feb. '04, Feb. '05, July '05, Feb. '06, July '06, Feb. '07.

When a contract is formed/validity of contract formation: 33%—July '05, July '06, Feb. '07, July '07, Feb. '09.

Valid offer: 33%—Feb. '04, July '04, Feb. '05, July '08, Feb. '09.

Valid acceptance: 27%—July '04, Feb. '05, July '08, Feb. '09.

Breach of contract: 33%—July '03, July '07, July '08, Feb. '09, July '09.

Statute of frauds: 27%—July '05, July '06, July '07, Feb. '09.

Doctrine of promissory estoppel: 27%—Feb. '05, July '06, July '07, Feb. '08.

Corporations

Director's duty of care: 73%—July '04, Feb. '05, July '05, Feb. '06, July '06, Feb. '07, July '07, Feb. '08, Feb. '09, July '09, Feb. '10.
Director's duty of loyalty: 53%—Feb. '05, July '05, Feb. '06, July '06, Feb. '07, July '07, Feb. '08, Feb. '09.
Legality of payment/nonpayment of dividends: 33%—July '05, Feb. '06, July '06, Feb. '08, Feb. '10.
Business Judgment Rule: 47%—July '05, Feb. '06, Feb. '07, Feb. '08, Feb. '09, July '09, Feb. '10.
Ultra Vires doctrine: 27%—July '04, Feb. '07, July '07, July '09.
Director's personal liability: 27%—Feb. '07, Feb. '09, July '09, Feb. '10.

Criminal Law

Accomplice liability: 60%—July '04, Feb. '05, July '05, July '06, Feb. '07, July '07, July '08, July '09, Feb. '10.
Aggravated assault: 33%—July '03, July '05, Feb. '06, July '07, July '08.
First degree murder: 27%—July '04, Feb. '07, Feb. '09, July '09.
Second degree murder: 27%—July '03, July '04, Feb. '07, July '09.
Manslaughter: 33%—July '03, Feb. '04, July '04, Feb. '07, July '09.
Negligent homicide: 33%—July '03, July '04, Feb. '07, July '08, July '09.
Felony Murder: 33%—Feb. '04, Feb. '05, July '06, July '07, Feb. '09.
Attempt: 40%—Feb. '05, July '06, Feb. '08, Feb. '09, July '09, Feb. '10.
Duress defense: 27%—July '05, July '06, Feb. '07, Feb. '10.
Theft: 27%—July '05, July '07, Feb. '10, July '10.

Criminal Procedure

Privilege against self incrimination: 33%—Feb. '06, July '06, Feb. '07, Feb. '09, July '09.
Miranda rights: 27%—Feb. '04, Feb. '05, Feb. '09, July '09.
Confrontation Clause: 27%—Feb. '06, Feb. '08, Feb. '09, July '09.

Evidence

Hearsay: 93%—July '03, Feb. '04, July '04, Feb. '05, July '05, Feb. '06, July '06, Feb. '07, July '07, Feb. '08, July '08, Feb. '09, July '09, Feb. '10.

Relevance: 80%—July '03, Feb. '04, Feb. '05, July '05, Feb. '06, July '06, Feb. '07, July '07, July '08, Feb. '09, July '09, Feb. '10.

Authentication: 67%—July '03, Feb. '04, July '04, July '05, Feb. '06, July '06, July '07, Feb. '08, July '08, July '09.

Admissibility of a prior conviction: 53%—Feb. '04, July '04, Feb. '06, July '06, Feb. '08, July '08, Feb. '09, July '09.

Best Evidence Rule: 33%—Feb. '06, Feb. '07, July '07, Feb. '08, July '09.

Character evidence: 47%—July '03, Feb. '04, July '04, July '05, July '06, Feb. '08, July '08.

Impeachment with a criminal conviction: 40%—Feb. '04, Feb. '05, July '05, Feb. '06, July '06, July '08.

Probative value versus potential unfair prejudice: 40%—July '03, July '04, Feb. '05, July '05, Feb. '06, July '06.

Professional Responsibility

Conflict of interest: 40%—July '04, July '05, July '06, Feb. '07, Feb. '08, Feb. '10.

Advertisement for legal services/improper advertising: 27%—July '03, July '05, Feb. '07, July '09.

Duty of confidentiality: 27%—Feb. '05, Feb. '06, July '06, Feb. '10.

Property

Recording Act: 40%—Feb. '04, July '05, Feb. '06, Feb. '08, Feb. '09, Feb. '10.

Creation of an easement: 33%—July '03, Feb. '04, Feb. '08, July '09, Feb. '10.

Easement by implication: 27%—July '03, Feb. '04, Feb. '08, July '09.

Easement by prescription: 27%—July '03, Feb. '04, Feb. '08, July '09.

Torts

Negligence: 80%—July '03, Feb. '04, July '04, Feb. '05, July '05, Feb. '07, July '07, Feb. '08, July '08, Feb. '09, July '09, Feb. '10.

Negligence per se: 40%—July '03, Feb. '05, July '05, Feb. '07, Feb. '08, July '08.

Actual cause: 27%—Feb. '08, Feb. '09, July '09, Feb. '10.

Proximate cause: 73%—July '04, Feb. '05, July '05, Feb. '06, Feb. '07, July '07, Feb. '08, July '08, Feb. '09, July '09, Feb. '10.

Comparative fault: 60%—July '03, Feb. '04, July '04, Feb. '05, July '05, Feb. '06, Feb. '08, July '08, Feb. '09.

Intervening or superseding causes: 53%—Feb. '04, Feb. '05, July '05, Feb. '06, Feb. '07, Feb. '08, Feb. '09, Feb. '10.

Foreseeability: 40%—July '03, Feb. '04, July '05, Feb. '06, Feb. '07, July '09.

Damages: 33%—July '04, July '06, Feb. '07, July '07, July '09.

Duty owed to trespasser: 27%—July '03, July '04, Feb. '07, Feb. '09.

Strict liability: 40%—July '03, Feb. '04, July '04, Feb. '06, July '07, Feb. '09.

Wills/Trusts

Validity of a will: 60%—July '03, July '05, July '06, Feb. '07, Feb. '08, July '08, Feb. '09, July '09, July '10.

Holographic will: 33%—July '05, July '06, Feb. '08, Feb. '09, July '10.

Anti-lapse statute: 27%—July '07, Feb. '08, Feb. '09, July '09.

Residuary: 33%—July '07, Feb. '08, Feb. '09, July '09, July '10.

Appendix C— Types of Questions No Longer on the MBE

A few side notes as they relate to the type of questions presented on the MBE. First, according to the NCBE, there are no longer "Roman Numeral" type questions on the MBE. I mention this because you will undoubtedly encounter many sample "Roman Numeral" questions in your practice materials—and they can be tricky. I'm not saying you shouldn't try to answer these types of practice questions, but know that you won't have to deal with them on the actual exam. Here is an example of a "Roman Numeral" question, just so you know what I'm talking about:

MBE SAMPLE QUESTION #8

> Able entered into a written contract with Baker to sell Greenacre. The contract was dated June 19 and called for a closing date on the following August 19. There was no other provision in the contract concerning the closing date. The contract contained the following clause: "subject to the purchaser, Baker, obtaining a satisfactory mortgage at the current rate." On the date provided for closing, Baker advised Able that he was unable to close because his mortgage application was still being processed by a bank. Able desired to declare the contract at an end and consulted his attorney in regard to his legal position.
>
> Which of the following are relevant in advising Able of his legal position?
>
> I. Is time of the essence?
> II. Parol evidence rule.
> III. Statute of Frauds.
> IV. Specific performance.

A. I and III only.
B. II and IV only.
C. II, III, and IV only.
D. I, II, III, and IV.

Additionally, the NCBE has phased out multiple questions based on a single fact pattern. At this point, it is a good bet that such questions are already phased out. Here is an example of how these type of questions are introduced: "Questions 31–32 are based on the following fact pattern." Now, instead of having multiple questions from one fact pattern, each question has its own fact pattern. It's okay to go ahead and do either of these types of questions in your practice sessions, but do know that they won't show up on the actual exam.

Appendix D— Recent Arizona Bar Exam Pass Rates[9]

Exam Date	Number of Applicants	% Pass
Feb. 2006	450	65.1
July 2005	758	67.5
Feb. 2005	384	66.7
July 2004	743	66.5
Feb. 2004	391	66
July 2003	656	72
Feb. 2003	365	58
July 2002	634	73
Feb. 2002	356	64
July 2001	590	75
Feb. 2001	323	66
July 2000	556	75
Feb. 2000	344	71
July 1999	584	75
Feb. 1999	350	75
July 1998	562	76

9. The information can be found at the Arizona State Supreme Court's Committee on Examination website at: http://www.supreme.state.az.us./admis/examinfo.htm (last visited on March 24, 2010).

Index